Soul Protectors

CH Jodi M Dehn

Published by Tamerlane Media, 2025.

SOUL PROTECTORS

First edition. January 17, 2025.

Copyright © 2025 CH Jodi M Dehn.

ISBN: 979-8989852420

Written by CH Jodi M Dehn.

REVIEWS

"Prepare to be taken to another empyrean domain...what a read! A thrilling read, with Jodi displaying an abundance of wisdom, knowledge, and thoughtfulness on issues and topics beyond our logic. Time to refresh on your top-down processing.".

Anthony Joseph Kerrigan, Angel talker – Kilkenny, Ireland

"When I first met Jodi, the first thing I said to her was that you are not from this plane nor from this earth. Jodi is a Pleiadian – when she speaks her words are like ancient wisdom. She was a wise soul from the moment she was born. Jodi to me is an Incoming Angel bringing with her all the celestial ancient knowledge. And also a very good friend."

Kathrine Sorilos, world renowned psychic medium – Athens, Greece

"Jodi's book is nothing short of a profound journey into the essence of the soul. With a lyrical and deeply personal style, she explores the mysteries of our being and the unseen forces guiding us. Her insights into alignment, authenticity, and the role of angels resonate on a level that feels both universal and intimately personal. This is not just a book—it's an experience that will leave you reflecting on your own soul's journey long after the final page. Truly transformative."

Shane Pittman, Holzer Files, 28 Days Haunted, Paranormal Mysteries, and co-owner of Beacon TV

INTRODUCTION

In the dimmest hours, when questions sneak in like whispers, we find ourselves grappling with one of humanity's oldest mysteries: What is the soul? Does it exist beyond the confines of our bodies, or is it woven into every fiber of our physical being, invisible but integral? These questions aren't just philosophical musings; they are markers of something deeply profound, a yearning to understand the essence of who we are.

If we're honest, the concept of the soul feels both distant and intensely personal. It is that part of us we can't fully define, yet feel keenly in moments of joy, pain, and even fear. In the quiet moments, this mystery seems almost to beckon us to explore it further, as if our own souls are reaching out for understanding.

Across centuries and cultures, people have sensed a guiding presence on this journey of exploration, often envisioning celestial beings—angels, spirits, guides—standing as protectors or companions to the soul. These figures show up in countless religious texts, myths, and spiritual teachings, each suggesting that we are not alone in this quest. They hint at a connection between our souls and the universe beyond, a whisper that there may be more to us than just the flesh and bone we see. What role do these beings play? Are they here to lead us toward enlightenment, to protect us, or simply to remind us that the soul's journey is never solitary?

Our souls are perhaps the most enigmatic aspects of our existence. They are rich with mystery and beauty, holding a vastness that defies definition. Imagine them as vessels of infinite potential, the birthplace of our deepest emotions, creativity, and the essence of who we are. It's the soul, after all, that fuels our capacity to love, to feel empathy, and to form connections with others.

This ability to bond deeply, to share and shape experiences with others, adds a layer of wonder to our lives. We create art, forge relationships, and find meaning in life's moments, all through this elusive entity that we can never quite capture.

In moments of connection—when a piece of music moves us to tears or a friend's embrace offers comfort in ways words cannot—our souls seem to transcend the boundaries of the physical. It's as if, in those moments, we brush against something vast, something timeless, leaving us with the sense that there's a part of us beyond logic or science. This ethereal quality of the soul is what gives life its richness and depth, turning ordinary moments into profound experiences and imbuing our lives with a uniquely human complexity.

Yet, for all its beauty, the soul can also be unsettling. It is elusive, slipping through the grasp of understanding like mist, prompting questions that echo through history. What is it, truly? Where does it reside? Will it continue beyond our physical lives, or is it bound to the here and now?

Philosophy, theology, and science have all ventured answers, yet none have captured it fully. The soul's intangible nature invites endless contemplation, drawing us into a search for answers that, like the horizon, seem to recede as we approach. It's this very mystery, this inability to pin down what the soul is, that stirs both wonder and frustration. We are, in a way, forever chasing our own essence.

But the soul isn't just a source of wonder; it can also evoke fear. The idea of an eternal essence within us raises questions we may not want to face. What if our souls are flawed? What if they carry, not just our love and joy, but the weight of our darkest thoughts and actions?

Many religions speak of judgment, of an afterlife where our souls are evaluated, and this idea can be terrifying. The fear that our souls might bear consequences we can't undo, that they might linger beyond this life, unsettles us on a primal level. And the unknown—what happens to the soul when the body dies—lurks like a shadow, tapping into a deep, ancient fear of what lies beyond.

Our souls, then, are a blend of excitement, mystery, and fear. They drive us to create, to seek understanding, and to confront the very questions that define existence. Each of us is a story written in the language of the soul, a tapestry of hopes, doubts, love, and curiosity. It is this rich complexity that makes the soul one of humanity's most profound mysteries, one that invites us—compels us—to seek answers even as they elude us.

And perhaps, in this search, we are guided by something unseen, something beyond ourselves. Maybe, just maybe, we are not alone on this journey.

AWAKENING THE ETERNAL SELF: SOUL AS CONSCIOUSNESS

As the human settled into the quiet of their thoughts, they spoke softly into the stillness. "Soul, I've been wondering... is my consciousness, this sense of being me, really just you? Are you what I've been calling my awareness all along?"

The soul's presence was warm, like a gentle current wrapping around the human's heart. "Yes," it replied, the voice soft but steady. "Your consciousness is the expression of me. It's the thread of awareness that ties your experiences, emotions, and identity together. Every time you think, 'I am,' you're speaking from the essence of your soul."

The human tilted their head, considering the answer. "So, all my thoughts, my memories, and my dreams—they're part of you?"

"More than that," the soul said. "They are me. I hold the depth of your emotions, the lessons you've learned, and the dreams you've carried through lifetimes. Your consciousness is the lens through which you experience the world, but I am the light shining through it. I am the continuity of you, beyond time, beyond the physical."

The human's brow furrowed. "But science says consciousness comes from the brain. Neurons firing, synapses connecting... Isn't that where it all begins?"

The soul's energy shimmered, as if smiling gently. "The brain is an instrument," it said. "A remarkable one, yes, but it is not the source. Think of it like a radio—it picks up the signal, but it doesn't create the music. I am the music, the eternal essence that plays through the instrument of your body and mind. Even when the radio is turned off, the music continues."

The human's thoughts wandered to moments of intuition, those sudden flashes of knowing without explanation. "Is that why sometimes I just know something? Or feel a pull toward something I can't explain?"

"Exactly," the soul replied, its tone brimming with quiet wisdom. "Those moments are when the veil between us thins, and you feel the truth of my presence. Intuition is my voice, guiding you, often with the help of higher beings. Archangel Raziel, for example, often works to help you access this hidden wisdom, opening doors to clarity when you trust in the unseen."

The human nodded slowly, recalling vivid dreams and moments of profound connection. "And what about when people have near-death experiences or feel like they've left their bodies? Is that me—my consciousness—stepping beyond the physical?"

"Precisely," the soul said, its warmth deepening. "When the body stills and the distractions of the physical fade, you see yourself for what you truly are—limitless and eternal. During these moments, Archangel Azrael often assists, gently guiding souls as they glimpse the vastness of their true essence. What you perceive as stepping out of your body is really you realizing that you were never confined by it in the first place."

The human exhaled, as if releasing a weight they hadn't known they carried. "So, if my consciousness is you, does that mean I... we... are immortal?"

"Yes, possibly" the soul whispered. "I have been with you long before this life and will continue long after. Each lifetime is a chapter in the story of your existence. Your body may be temporary, but I—your essence—am eternal. I carry your wisdom, your love, and your growth forward, weaving them into the greater tapestry of who you are becoming."

A quiet awe settled over the human. "And yet, even though I'm unique, you're saying I'm also connected to something bigger?"

"Beautifully so," the soul said. "Each of us is a thread in the infinite fabric of the universe. You are distinct, yes, but never separate. Every soul resonates with the collective, just as each star contributes its light to the night sky. Archangel Metatron, who bridges the human and the divine, often reminds us of this truth: we are all part of one great whole, and yet each of us shines uniquely."

The human leaned forward, resting their chin in their hands. "But why? Why do I get to experience this individuality if I'm also part of everything else?"

"Because that is the gift," the soul said tenderly. "To experience the universe from your own perspective, to learn, to grow, to love deeply. Your individuality allows you to see the divine in the details, while your connection reminds you that you are never truly alone. Together, these truths create the balance of existence."

The human let the words wash over them, feeling a sense of quiet reverence. "So, if my consciousness is you, what does that mean for how I should live my life?"

"It means living in alignment with your true self," the soul answered. "Listen to the quiet whispers of your intuition. Honor your inner voice. Seek what brings you joy and peace, for those are the paths where I shine brightest. Remember that each choice ripples outward, shaping not just your journey but the collective symphony we all belong to."

"And what about when life ends?" the human asked softly. "What happens then?"

The soul's presence enveloped them, warm and steady. "Death is not an end," it said. "It is a doorway, a return to the fullness of your being. Your consciousness—your soul—continues, carrying all you have learned into the next chapter. Archangel Azrael walks with us in these moments, ensuring that the transition is one of grace and peace. You will not lose yourself. Instead, you will become more fully who you have always been."

The human closed their eyes, breathing deeply. "So, my consciousness is both me and something much greater."

"Yes," the soul replied. "You are the spark and the fire, the wave and the ocean. You are the melody and the symphony, ever unique and ever connected. And as you embrace this truth, you will live with a deeper grace, knowing you are part of something eternal and endlessly beautiful."

In the stillness that followed, the human felt a profound peace—a quiet certainty that their journey, no matter how winding, was guided by something infinite. And in that moment, they understood: their consciousness was not just theirs. It was the song of their soul, echoing across lifetimes, part of a harmony that stretched beyond time.

STORY: THE LIBRARY OF SHADOWS

It was a stormy night when Evelyn stumbled upon the ancient library tucked away in a forgotten corner of her grandmother's estate. The mansion itself was a relic of the past, with creaking floors and towering ceilings that seemed to whisper secrets from another era. Evelyn, a curious and introspective young woman, had always felt a deep connection to the old house, as if it held the key to something profound within her.

As the rain pelted against the windows, she wandered through the dusty corridors, her steps guided by an inexplicable pull. She found herself standing before a grand, ornate door she had never noticed before. With a sense of both trepidation and excitement, she turned the brass handle and entered.

The library was unlike any she had ever seen. Shelves lined with leather-bound books stretched to the ceiling, and in the center of the room stood a massive oak table, its surface cluttered with ancient manuscripts and curious artifacts. A faint, ethereal glow emanated from a crystal chandelier overhead, casting dancing shadows on the walls.

Drawn to the table, Evelyn noticed an old journal bound in deep blue leather. She opened it to find pages filled with delicate, flowing script. As she began to read, she realized this was not just any journal—it was the diary of her great-grandmother, Eliza, a woman rumored to have been deeply in tune with the spiritual and mystical.

Eliza's journal recounted her own experiences with the soul, consciousness, and the subconscious mind. It spoke of visions and dreams, of guidance from realms beyond the physical. Evelyn was particularly struck by a passage where Eliza described a series of vivid dreams she had, dreams that seemed to be messages from her soul, influenced by both her conscious and subconscious mind.

"The soul," Eliza wrote, "is a vessel of light, guided by the conscious mind's clarity and the subconscious mind's depth. It is in the interplay of these realms that we find our true path."

As Evelyn read further, she discovered that Eliza had been on a quest to understand the nature of her own soul, a quest that led her to uncover hidden truths about their family and their connection to the mystical.

That night, Evelyn fell into a deep sleep, her mind swirling with the mysteries of the journal. In her dreams, she found herself in a vast, ethereal landscape, where the boundaries between conscious thought and subconscious imagery blurred. She stood at the edge of a forest, a place both familiar and strange.

A figure emerged from the shadows, a woman with kind eyes and a serene presence—it was Eliza. "Evelyn," she spoke softly, "your journey is just beginning. You must learn to listen to the whispers of your soul, for they will guide you to truths hidden in the depths of your mind."

Over the following weeks, Evelyn immersed herself in the journal, uncovering layers of wisdom and insight. She practiced meditation, allowing herself to delve into her subconscious mind, where dreams and visions began to unfold more frequently. Each vision brought messages that were both cryptic and illuminating, urging her to explore the hidden chambers of her own psyche.

One night, as she meditated by the fireplace, Evelyn experienced a vision more vivid than any before. She saw a labyrinth, its pathways winding and intricate. At the center of the labyrinth stood a mirror, and in the mirror, she saw herself—only, it was an older version of her, eyes filled with wisdom and compassion.

"Your soul's purpose is not a destination, but a journey," the reflection spoke. "It is guided by the choices you make in your conscious mind and the truths revealed by your subconscious. Trust in the process, and you will find your way.

Evelyn's journey led her to discover family secrets long buried. She learned of a hidden lineage of women in her family, all of whom had been guardians of spiritual knowledge. Her great-grandmother Eliza had been the last in line, and now, it was Evelyn's turn to continue the legacy.

With each revelation, Evelyn felt her soul expanding, guided by the harmony between her conscious decisions and the insights from her subconscious mind. She realized that the library was not just a repository of knowledge but a gateway to understanding the depths of her own being.

In the end, Evelyn embraced her role as a guardian of the mystical, understanding that the soul's journey is one of balance. The conscious mind provides direction and clarity, while the subconscious mind offers depth and wisdom. Together, they guide the soul through the labyrinth of life, illuminating the path with each step.

As she sat by the fireplace, journal in hand, Evelyn felt a sense of peace and purpose. She knew that the journey of the soul was ongoing, an ever-unfolding mystery that she was now equipped to navigate with grace and insight. The library's shadows no longer whispered secrets but sang of the harmonious dance between consciousness and the subconscious, guiding her towards her true self.

And so, in the quiet of the ancient mansion, amidst the flickering firelight, Evelyn's soul shone brightly, a testament to the profound journey of self-discovery and the eternal dance of the mind's realms.

STORY: THE CELESTIAL MYSTERY: ANGELS, SOULS AND THE UNIVERSE

The small town of Glenshire was the kind of place where mysteries didn't happen. Or at least, that's what everyone thought until Reverend Elias Whitaker vanished without a trace. The reverend, known for his wisdom and kindness, left behind nothing but his old, leather-bound journal and whispers of strange celestial visions.

Detective Claire Sullivan was called in to investigate. Claire was known for her sharp intuition and an uncanny ability to see beyond the obvious. As she entered the reverend's modest home, she was immediately drawn to his study, a room filled with ancient books and artifacts from different faiths and philosophies.

On his desk lay the journal, opened to a page that spoke of angels, souls, and the vast universe. Claire settled into his worn armchair, flipping through the pages filled with meticulously detailed notes and musings.

The journal entries were a blend of theology, philosophy, and personal reflections. Reverend Whitaker had been deeply engrossed in the nature of the soul, the role of angels, and the interconnectedness of the universe.

The Soul: Whitaker believed the soul was a spark of divine light, eternal and boundless. His writings echoed ancient teachings, describing the soul as a traveler through realms, guided by higher beings.

Angels: According to Whitaker, angels were celestial messengers, tasked with guiding souls and maintaining the cosmic balance. He wrote about their role in helping souls navigate life's struggles and traumas, providing comfort and insight.

The Universe: Whitaker's entries often veered into the cosmic, describing the universe as a grand tapestry woven with the threads of countless souls. He saw the universe as a living entity, pulsating with the energy of every soul that ever existed.

One entry caught Claire's eye:

"On the night of the celestial alignment, the veil between worlds thins. Angels whisper truths that transcend human understanding, guiding souls to their destined paths. I feel it approaching—something beyond our grasp, a mystery of the divine."

Claire's investigation led her to Father Michael, a close friend of Reverend Whitaker and a scholar of celestial phenomena. Father Michael revealed that the reverend had been preparing for a rare celestial alignment, an event that many believed could open gateways to other realms.

"Elias was convinced that this alignment would reveal profound truths about our existence," Father Michael said, his voice tinged with both awe and concern. "He believed it would provide a glimpse into the divine order of the universe."

That night, Claire ventured to the old observatory on the outskirts of Glenshire, where Reverend Whitaker often spent his nights stargazing. The alignment was already in motion, the night sky alive with brilliant constellations and shimmering lights.

As she watched, Claire felt a strange sensation, as if the very fabric of reality was shifting. She heard a faint, melodic whisper—a celestial symphony that seemed to emanate from the stars themselves.

Suddenly, a figure appeared in the observatory—a being of light, radiating warmth and serenity. Claire's breath caught in her throat as she realized she was in the presence of an angel. The angel spoke in a voice that was both gentle and powerful, resonating deep within her soul.

"Do not be afraid, Claire. You are closer to the truth than you realize. Reverend Whitaker has crossed into a realm where souls and angels coexist in harmony, a place where the mysteries of the universe unfold."

Claire's mind raced. "Where is he? Can I bring him back?"

The angel smiled. "He is where he is meant to be, understanding the divine order and aiding souls in their journeys. Your path, Claire, is to continue his work, to uncover and share these truths with those who seek them."

In the weeks that followed, Claire delved deeper into Reverend Whitaker's notes, combining them with her own observations and the insights from her angelic encounter. She began to write about the interconnectedness of the soul, angels, and the universe, sharing these revelations with the people of Glenshire and beyond.

Her writings spoke of the soul's eternal journey, guided by angels who provided strength and wisdom. She described the universe as a living entity, a cosmic dance of energy and light where every soul played a part.

Claire's work inspired many to look beyond the mundane, to seek a deeper understanding of their own souls and their place in the universe. She often returned to the observatory, feeling the presence of Reverend Whitaker and the angels, knowing that she was never truly alone.

Years later, Claire's writings became a cornerstone of modern spiritual thought, bridging the gap between ancient wisdom and contemporary understanding. The mystery of Reverend Whitaker's disappearance remained, but his legacy lived on through Claire's work.

The town of Glenshire, once a quiet place of ordinary lives, became a beacon for seekers of truth, drawn by the celestial mystery that began with a reverend's journal and a detective's unyielding quest for answers. And as the stars continued their eternal dance, the whispers of angels guided countless souls on their journey through the cosmos.

CHAPTER: THE WHISPER OF THE SOUL: CONVERSATIONS BEYOND THE VEIL

"Do you ever feel like I'm trying to talk to you?" the soul asked, its voice gentle yet persistent, like the soft murmur of wind through trees.

The human paused, caught off guard by the thought. "Sometimes... I guess I do. But it's hard to tell. It's more like a feeling than a voice. Is that you?"

"Always," the soul replied, the tone infused with warmth. "I'm always here. It's just that you're often too distracted to notice."

The human sighed, setting down the book they were half-reading. "You're not wrong. So... how do you communicate? And what do you want me to know?"

The soul smiled inwardly. "I whisper through intuition. That gut feeling you get, the one that nudges you toward or away from something—that's me. It's subtle, I know, but powerful if you listen."

"Intuition..." the human mused. "You mean those moments when something feels right or wrong without a clear reason?"

"Exactly," the soul affirmed. "Like the time you turned down that job offer that seemed perfect on paper but felt all wrong. You trusted me then, and it led you to something far better."

The human nodded slowly, a flicker of recognition sparking. "Okay, that makes sense. What else?"

"Dreams," the soul continued. "When you're asleep, your mind is quiet enough for me to speak more clearly. The symbols, the emotions—those are my way of guiding you or revealing truths you might not see in waking life."

The human leaned forward, intrigued. "But dreams can be so random. How do I know which ones are important?"

"You'll feel it," the soul assured. "Some dreams linger, don't they? They stay with you, vivid and insistent. Those are the ones you should pay attention to."

"Alright," the human said. "What about those weird coincidences? Like seeing the same number everywhere or a song playing at just the right moment. Is that you, too?"

"Sometimes," the soul replied. "But often, most of these messages come from angels."

The human blinked. "Angels? They're real?"

The soul chuckled softly. "Very much so. They're here to help, just like I am. They amplify my messages, send signs, and protect you."

"Wait," the human interrupted. "How do I tell the difference between you and them?"

"Good question," the soul said. "My whispers are more internal—a feeling, a knowing. Angels, though... they like to get creative. Ever notice repeating numbers, like 111 or 444?"

The human's eyes widened. "Yes! I see 222 all the time. It's eerie."

"That's them," the soul said. "Numbers are one of their favorite ways to communicate. Each sequence has a meaning. For example, 222 often means balance and alignment. It's their way of nudging you toward harmony."

"And feathers," the human said suddenly. "I've found white feathers in the strangest places."

The soul smiled. "Another calling card of the angels. Feathers, butterflies, rainbows—symbols of lightness, protection, and divine presence."

The human hesitated, then asked, "Have I ever... heard them? Or you?"

"Yes," the soul said softly. "Remember that moment when you were so lost, and a calm, loving voice said, 'Keep going; you're not alone'? That was them. Their voices are pure love, gentle but unmistakable."

The human's throat tightened. "I remember. It felt... safe."

"Exactly," the soul said. "They're always near. And when you quiet your mind—through meditation, prayer, or simply being still—you make space to hear them and me more clearly."

"But how do I know I'm not imagining it all?" the human whispered.

The soul's voice grew tender. "By the way it feels. Truth resonates. When you hear or feel a message that fills you with peace, hope, or clarity, that's real. Trust it."

The human exhaled deeply, their shoulders relaxing. "Okay, so how do I get better at this? At listening to you and them?"

"Start by being present," the soul suggested. "Mindfulness helps you notice the subtle signs and feelings. Create moments of stillness—a sacred space where you can focus inward."

"Like meditation?" the human asked.

"Yes," the soul said. "Meditation, journaling, or even just sitting in nature. Write down what you feel or notice. Sometimes, the act of writing reveals messages you didn't realize were there."

"And I can just... ask for guidance?" the human ventured.

"Always," the soul replied. "Angels and I are here to help, but we respect your free will. Ask, and we'll respond in the ways you're most likely to notice."

The human smiled faintly. "And what if I get it wrong? Misinterpret something?"

The soul's voice was warm with reassurance. "Then we'll try again. We're patient. Look for patterns, confirmations—like hearing the same message in different ways. And if you're ever unsure, just ask for clarity."

The human sat quietly for a moment, the weight of the conversation settling into their heart. "So... you're saying I'm never really alone?"

"Never," the soul said firmly. "I am you, and angels surround you. Together, we guide, protect, and inspire you. All you need to do is listen."

THREADS OF ESSENCE:
UNRAVELING SOUL AND SPIRIT

The human sat quietly, gazing into the endless expanse of their inner world, searching for clarity. The questions had been forming for weeks, whispers of curiosity that would not be silenced. What truly defines us? What distinguishes the soul from the spirit? Finally, they reached out to their soul, hoping for answers.

"I've been wondering," the human began, their voice steady yet laced with longing. "What's the difference between the soul and the spirit? People speak of them as if they're the same, but something tells me they're not."

The soul, patient and luminous, responded gently, "Ah, my dear, you've touched upon one of the great mysteries of existence. Let us explore this together, for understanding this difference can open doors to deeper self-awareness and connection with the divine."

The human leaned in closer, as if proximity would make the answers clearer. "Start with the soul. What are you to me?"

"I am your essence," the soul said. "I am the core of who you are—your unique identity that carries the memories, lessons, and emotions of your journey across lifetimes. I am the part of you that weeps in sorrow, rejoices in love, and dreams of infinite possibilities. When you paint, sing, or pour your heart into a passion, that is me expressing myself through you."

The human smiled, the answer resonating deeply. "So, you're the part of me that feels connected to my purpose, that holds onto the lessons I've learned?"

"Yes," the soul replied, its presence warm like the glow of a distant sun. "And yet, I am more. I am timeless. I existed before you were born into this life, and I will continue long after this chapter ends. I am the thread that weaves your many lifetimes into one grand tapestry.

Archangel Jeremiel often works with souls like us, helping to review and reflect on these experiences during moments of transformation or in dreams."

The human's brow furrowed slightly. "And the spirit? How does it fit into all this?"

"Ah, the spirit," the soul said, its tone reverent now. "The spirit is the breath of life, the divine spark that animates your being. It is the energy that flows through you, connecting you to the Source of all creation. Imagine it as the current that powers the vessel of your body and the canvas of your soul. Without the spirit, there would be no life, no movement, no vitality."

"Then the spirit is universal?" the human asked.

"Precisely," the soul affirmed. "While I am uniquely yours, shaped by your experiences and individuality, the spirit is a shared force, part of the universal energy that flows through all living things. Archangel Metatron, the keeper of sacred knowledge, often works with the spirit to connect you to divine wisdom, guiding you to transcendence and higher understanding."

The human closed their eyes, letting the words sink in. "So, the spirit is what ties me to the divine, while you, the soul, are what makes me... me."

"Exactly," the soul said. "But remember, we are not separate. We work together in harmony. I, the soul, provide the depth, the emotions, and the individuality. The spirit infuses us with life, purpose, and the connection to something far greater. Together, we create the beautiful interplay that is your existence."

The human thought for a moment, their mind turning to various teachings. "Different traditions seem to speak of the soul and spirit in their own ways. Are they describing this same relationship?"

"They are," the soul replied, "though each uses its own language. Western philosophy often sees the soul as the seat of emotions and intellect, as thinkers like Plato described it—the essence of a person. In

Eastern traditions, such as Hinduism, the soul is the Atman, the eternal self, while the spirit is akin to the life force that connects all beings to the universal Brahman. Indigenous beliefs see the soul as a unique essence that journeys across lifetimes, while the spirit is the life force present in all of nature, binding every being in an interconnected web."

The human nodded slowly, the pieces falling into place. "It feels like everything—my emotions, my purpose, my life—is a blend of the two. Is that right?"

The soul glowed brighter in acknowledgment. "Yes. This blend is your holistic existence. In your daily life, the spirit sustains you, giving you vitality and the capacity to connect with the divine. I, your soul, guide you with the wisdom of your experiences, helping you find meaning and navigate your path. Together, we invite you to evolve, to grow, and to understand your role in the grand design."

"And when life ends?" the human whispered.

"Upon death," the soul said softly, "the spirit returns to the universal Source, the great river of energy from which it came. I, the soul, continue the journey, carrying the lessons of this life forward. Archangel Azrael, the angel of transitions, often helps guide this passage, ensuring that your spirit finds peace and your soul moves forward in its divine plan."

The human opened their eyes, looking at the world around them with new depth. "It's all so beautiful. Knowing this... it changes how I see myself, my challenges, and my connection to the divine."

"Understanding this interplay," the soul said, "helps you honor both your individuality and your connection to the greater whole. When you meditate or pray, you nurture both of us—your soul and your spirit—deepening your self-awareness and aligning with divine energy. Call upon the angels, for they are always ready to guide you, to remind you of this truth."

The human smiled, a quiet peace settling over them. "Thank you. I feel... more whole now."

And in that moment, as the soul's light surrounded them and the unseen presence of angels whispered through the ether, the human felt the dance of soul and spirit—a timeless, divine harmony that brought depth to their individuality and connection to all of existence.

STORY: THE SOUL AND THE SPIRIT: A MYSTERY UNFOLDS

The town of Celestine was a place where mysteries lingered like morning fog, weaving through the streets and whispering through the trees. Nestled between dense forests and rolling hills, it was a town where the boundaries between the earthly and the ethereal seemed to blur. And it was here that an enigmatic story began told.

It all started with the disappearance of an old man named Elias Grey. Elias was a local legend, known for his deep knowledge of ancient lore and mystical practices. He lived in an old, creaky house on the outskirts of town, surrounded by books and artifacts that told stories of times long past. His presence was a comforting constant in Celestine, and when he vanished, the town felt an unsettling void.

Detective Jane Hart was called in to investigate. Jane was a sharp, intuitive detective with a knack for unraveling the most perplexing cases. But this one felt different. As she entered Elias's house, she was struck by an overwhelming sense of stillness, as if time itself had paused in anticipation.

The house was filled with books on spirituality, the soul, and the spirit. As Jane sifted through the volumes, she found a journal, its pages filled with Elias's meticulous handwriting. The journal spoke of his lifelong quest to understand the difference between the soul and the spirit. Intrigued, Jane delved deeper into his notes, hoping to find a clue to his whereabouts.

Elias's journal revealed that he believed the soul and the spirit were two distinct yet interconnected parts of human existence. He wrote about the soul as the essence of one's identity, carrying memories, emotions, and personal experiences. The spirit, on the other hand, was the life force, the divine spark that connected individuals to the universe and the divine.

One entry caught Jane's attention. Elias had written about a place called the "Astral Nexus," a hidden spot in the forest where he believed the veil between the soul and the spirit was thinnest. He described it as a place where one could commune with the divine and gain profound insights into their true nature.

Jane decided to explore this Astral Nexus, hoping it might hold the key to Elias's disappearance. As she ventured into the forest, guided by the journal's cryptic directions, she felt a strange energy in the air, as if the trees themselves were whispering secrets.

After hours of searching, Jane stumbled upon a clearing bathed in ethereal light. It was breathtaking, with ancient trees forming a natural circle around a shimmering pool of water. The air was thick with a sense of timelessness, and Jane felt a shiver of anticipation.

She approached the pool, peering into its depths. The water was so clear it seemed to vanish, revealing a reflective surface that mirrored the sky above. Jane felt an overwhelming urge to touch the water, and as she did, a vision unfolded before her eyes.

She saw Elias standing by the pool, speaking to a radiant figure—an angel. The angel was luminous, its presence exuding peace and wisdom. Elias and the angel were deep in conversation, discussing the nature of the soul and the spirit. The vision faded, leaving Jane with a sense of awe and a burning question: What had Elias discovered here?

As Jane pondered her next move, she felt a soft, warm light envelop her. Turning, she saw the angel from her vision. It was Seraphiel, Elias's celestial guide.

"Elias sought the truth about the soul and the spirit," Seraphiel said in a voice that resonated with the essence of the universe. "He understood that the soul is our unique essence, the repository of our personal experiences, while the spirit is the divine breath, the life force that connects us to the cosmos."

Jane listened intently as Seraphiel continued. "Elias has transcended the earthly realm to explore these mysteries further. He is safe, learning, and growing in the celestial planes. He wanted you to find this place, Jane, to understand the journey of the soul and the spirit."

Jane felt a profound sense of relief and understanding. Elias hadn't vanished—he had simply moved beyond the physical realm to continue his quest. Seraphiel's words resonated deeply within her, illuminating the intricate dance between the soul and the spirit.

With newfound clarity, Jane returned to Celestine, bringing with her a sense of peace and understanding. She shared her experience with the townsfolk, explaining Elias's journey and the profound truths he had discovered.

The town of Celestine became a place of spiritual exploration, with people flocking to the Astral Nexus to seek their own understanding of the soul and the spirit. Jane continued her work as a detective, but with a deeper appreciation for the mysteries that lay beyond the physical world.

In the end, Elias's disappearance was not a loss but a transformation. His journey into the realms of the soul and the spirit had opened a gateway for others to explore their own divine connections. And as Jane gazed up at the starry sky, she felt a profound sense of interconnectedness, knowing that the dance between the soul and the spirit was an eternal, beautiful mystery, guiding us all towards deeper understanding and enlightenment.

STORY: THE ENIGMA OF THE ETERNAL SOUL: A PHILOSOPHICAL MYSTERY

In the quiet town of Eldridge, nestled between rolling hills and ancient forests, mysteries were as common as the morning fog. But none intrigued the residents more than the recent disappearance of Professor Nathaniel Graves, a renowned philosopher known for his obsession with the origins of the soul.

Detective Evelyn Harper, a sharp-witted investigator with a penchant for solving the unsolvable, was called to the scene. Nathaniel's study was a labyrinth of books, scrolls, and manuscripts, each corner filled with the scent of old parchment and ink. Evelyn's eyes fell upon an ancient manuscript lying open on Nathaniel's desk. The title, written in elegant script, read: "The Enigma of the Eternal Soul."

Evelyn began her investigation by delving into Nathaniel's extensive notes. He had meticulously documented the perspectives of various philosophical traditions on the soul's origin.

Nathaniel had explored Plato's idea that the soul preexists the body, originating from the realm of Forms—a divine, immutable realm. He had noted how the soul, according to Plato, carries the memory of these perfect Forms.

Next, she found Aristotle's hylomorphism, where the soul and body form a single substance. The soul, as the essence of life, gives form to the body. Nathaniel seemed particularly fascinated by Aristotle's idea of the rational soul unique to humans.

The notes on Descartes highlighted the sharp separation between the mind (soul) and the body, with the soul being a non-material, thinking substance. Evelyn could almost hear Nathaniel's voice pondering the interaction between the immaterial and material.

SOUL PROTECTORS

Sartre and Heidegger's existential musings were next. Nathaniel had scribbled passionate notes about Sartre's idea that existence precedes essence, meaning the soul is crafted through choices and actions. Heidegger's focus on authenticity and being-in-the-world added another layer of complexity.

Kant and Hegel's philosophies revealed a more abstract view. Nathaniel had written about Kant's transcendental self, the noumenal essence beyond physical experience, and Hegel's Absolute Spirit, where individual souls are parts of a universal consciousness evolving towards self-realization.

Nathaniel's analysis of reductionist and eliminative materialism showed his struggle with these ideas. The notion that the soul could be entirely reduced to brain processes and neurological functions seemed at odds with his quest.

Lastly, Nathaniel had explored Vedanta and Taoism. The concept of Atman as the eternal self, identical with Brahman in Vedanta, and the Taoist idea of aligning the soul with the Tao, fascinated him. He seemed captivated by the idea of the soul's journey towards liberation and harmony.

Evelyn's curiosity was then piqued when she found a map tucked within the manuscript, leading to a secluded spot in the forest known as the Sanctuary of Souls. Following the map, she ventured into the dense woods, the air thick with the scent of pine and earth. After hours of trekking, she arrived at a clearing bathed in a mystical light. In the center stood an ancient stone altar covered in carvings representing various philosophical symbols.

As Evelyn approached the altar, she felt a strange energy envelop her. It was as if the thoughts and beliefs of countless philosophers were converging in this one sacred space. She noticed a small, intricately carved box on the altar. Opening it, she found a crystal orb glowing with an otherworldly light.

As Evelyn touched the orb, visions flooded her mind. She saw Nathaniel standing in the same clearing, conversing with ethereal figures that represented the various philosophical perspectives he had studied. Plato, Aristotle, Descartes, Sartre, Kant, Hegel, and even Eastern sages appeared, their discussions intertwining into a complex tapestry of thought.

Nathaniel had discovered that the Sanctuary of Souls was a place where the boundaries between these philosophies blurred, revealing deeper truths. The orb seemed to act as a conduit for accessing the collective wisdom of these great thinkers. Nathaniel's disappearance was not a vanishing but a transcendence into a higher realm of understanding.

Evelyn returned to Eldridge, her mind awash with the profound insights she had gained. She knew she couldn't explain Nathaniel's exact fate to the townsfolk, but she shared the essence of his journey—that he had transcended physical existence to explore the very origins of the soul.

The Sanctuary of Souls became a place of pilgrimage for seekers of wisdom, each hoping to catch a glimpse of the eternal truths Nathaniel had uncovered. Evelyn, too, found herself returning to the clearing, drawn by the mysteries it held and the eternal quest for understanding that it inspired.

In the end, the story of Nathaniel Graves and the Enigma of the Eternal Soul reminded everyone in Eldridge—and beyond—that the search for the soul's origins is a journey that transcends time, space, and even our physical existence. It is a quest that invites us to explore the depths of our own being, to embrace the wisdom of the ages, and to seek the eternal truths that lie beyond the veil of the material world.

CHAPTER: ORIGINS OF 'US' AND OUR CELESTIAL COMPANIONS

In a quiet room filled with the gentle scent of cedar, sage, and a faint echo of drumming, a dialogue began—a conversation as ancient as starlight. The air was rich with understanding, an unspoken thread between two presences who had journeyed through lifetimes together.

The human asked softly, "Where do you come from? I feel your presence here with me, but I don't remember how we started walking this path together."

The soul responded, "I come from a place beyond what you know as time or place, from the same source as the stars, the earth, the ancestors. In many stories, I am known by different names. In Native American traditions, for example, I am connected to the Great Spirit and to the spirits of animals, the land, and the sky. Across cultures, I am seen as part of nature's cycle. You and I are both woven from the essence of all that exists, part of a vast and eternal whole."

The human's curiosity deepened. "So many stories across the world talk about souls and beings from beyond. I've read about the Hindu Akashic Records, about ancestral spirits in Native traditions, and even about ancient beings, possibly extra-terrestrial beings, like the Anunnaki. Do all these stories carry some truth?"

The soul's voice was calm. "Each story holds a piece of truth. Every culture has glimpsed the divine and shaped it in ways they could understand. The Akashic Records, for instance, are real—an ethereal record of experiences, like the collective memory of the universe. Indigenous groups, too, speak of the wisdom of the ancestors, a lineage of knowledge passed through generations. Think of these records as a cosmic library, or as the spirits remembered in chants, dances, and stories—an archive that records the journey of every soul."

The human took this in, comforted by the thought of such a vast memory. "So the Akashic Records are real? And the memories of ancestors too? I can connect to them?"

"Yes," replied the soul. "Though it's less a place you visit physically and more of a connection you tune into. Through meditation, prayer, or ceremony, you can touch the wisdom there. Angels, or what some call 'devas,' often help souls access these insights. In Native American and other Indigenous traditions, ancestors and spirit guides play a similar role, helping you see what lies beyond your immediate life, and offering guidance."

The human's mind raced with connections. "So, devas and angels and spirit guides—are they similar in their roles, acting as protectors and intermediaries?"

"Precisely," the soul replied. "In Hindu tradition, devas are beings of light, helping to guide and protect, much like angels. In Native traditions, spirit guides may come in the form of animal spirits or the spirits of elders, each offering wisdom. They help you connect to your purpose and see beyond the boundaries of everyday life. Their wisdom can inspire, helping you to recognize your path."

The human's voice grew thoughtful. "And what about the Anunnaki, the beings from Mesopotamian stories who were said to have created humanity? Could they also be seen as guides?"

The soul's voice was steady. "The Anunnaki are indeed fascinating. In ancient Mesopotamian beliefs, they were seen as both creators and overseers. Their role as powerful beings who watched over humanity is echoed in the spirit beings of many cultures. In Indigenous groups, there are often stories of celestial beings or extra-terrestrials or star people—ancestors from beyond our world. While the origins of each myth vary, the essence is shared: beings from higher realms who guard and guide humanity."

SOUL PROTECTORS

The human looked down, almost as if reflecting on an ancient memory. "It's amazing how so many cultures have beings to guide or protect souls. Why is that?"

The soul's response was gentle. "Because each soul, though powerful, is still vulnerable as it journeys through existence. Many cultures' stories of angels, spirit guides, or animal spirits reflect this need for connection, for guidance on the unknown paths of life. The Egyptians, for instance, had the concepts of the 'ka' and 'ba'—parts of the soul watched over by gods like Osiris. And many Indigenous groups, too, believe in the presence of animal spirits or ancestor spirits, protecting and guiding us, ensuring we find peace, connection, and protection as we walk our paths."

The human felt the weight of this universal need for connection. "It's comforting to think of a guide or protector for the soul. I know in Jewish mysticism, angels are also seen as protectors, right?"

"Yes," the soul answered. "In Judaism, the soul is often seen in layers—the 'nefesh,' 'ruach,' and 'neshamah'—each connected to the divine. Angels are there to protect and guide souls through each stage. Archangels like Michael and Gabriel serve as protectors, helping each soul reach its potential. And Indigenous cultures, too, have guides, whether seen as angels, ancestral spirits, or animals. They are all present to help souls navigate life."

The human thought about this, a quiet understanding dawning. "So angels aren't only protectors but also teachers, just like the guides in Native traditions."

"Yes," the soul affirmed. "In Jewish thought, as in Indigenous traditions, guides bring lessons, sometimes through challenges, to help souls grow. They encourage you toward your highest self, showing you how to live in balance with yourself and the world."

The human's gaze softened. "That sounds like the guardian angels in Christianity too, there to protect, guide, and help us find our purpose."

"Yes, in Christianity, angels serve as messengers, protectors, and guides," the soul explained. "Guardian angels are assigned to individuals, reflecting each soul's value. Archangel Chamuel handles the protection and healing of our emotions where Archangel Zadkiel keeps our discernment abilities in tune. Across cultures, these guides connect the earthly and the divine, each in their own way."

The human's voice grew quiet with awe. "And in Islam, angels are there from the beginning, guiding the soul into life."

The soul nodded. "Yes, in Islam, the soul, or 'ruh,' is seen as a divine trust. Angels are there from the very beginning, offering guidance. Guardian angels, or 'malaikah,' record each thought and action. They serve as both protectors and witnesses, aligning the soul with its purpose and reminding it of its connection to the divine."

The human took this in, sensing the unity in these traditions. "All these beings—angels, devas, spirit guides—are they all part of something bigger? Part of this divine tapestry?"

The soul's voice was warm and steady. "Exactly. They are threads in a larger design, just as you and I are. Every soul, every guide, is connected, each playing a role in the ongoing creation of the universe. These beings remind humanity that even on life's most solitary paths, no soul is truly alone."

The human felt a deep peace settle in. "So, this journey of the soul—it never really ends, does it? It just keeps unfolding?"

The soul replied, with a warmth that filled the room. "It is both endless and ever-evolving. Some souls may reach a place where they merge back into the divine source, while others continue to journey, to learn, to grow. Each experience, each life, is a step along this path. One day, perhaps, as your understanding deepens, you may find that you, too, become a guide for others."

The human breathed in deeply, as though savoring this thought. "So the angels, the devas, the animal spirits—they're not only here to help us, but to show us what we might become."

"Yes," said the soul. "They remind you of the potential within yourself. They are companions, helping you see your own connection to the divine. Across cultures and lifetimes, these stories endure because they reflect a fundamental truth: we are all part of something greater, a journey toward understanding, unity, and compassion."

As their conversation quieted, a sense of peace filled the room. The human felt as though, in these shared words, the mysteries of existence had grown both simpler and deeper. The soul and its human companion had woven a tapestry of understanding—a glimpse into the infinite that lay within. And for now, that was enough.

CHAPTER: DIVINE CONNECTION: THE BOND BETWEEN SOUL AND ANGELS

In a quiet space, the human sat, deeply reflective, listening to their soul's words as it began speaking of Gabriel and Michael. The air seemed to hold a subtle reverence as they explored these ancient figures, whose presence reached across time and cultures, touching something profound within the journey of every soul.

The soul explained that Gabriel and Michael were more than distant beings; they embodied universal qualities that lived within every person. "Gabriel is the voice of revelation," it said softly, "the one who brings clarity and truth when you need it most. Michael, on the other hand, is your inner strength, the courage that rises up to help you hold onto that truth, especially in moments of challenge."

The human nodded slowly, feeling the truth of these words sink in. They had always admired the stories of Gabriel and Michael—archangels described in ancient texts across Judaism, Christianity, and Islam. But these figures had felt remote, mythic. Now, the soul's words brought them closer, turning them into energies they could recognize within themselves.

"What makes Gabriel the one who brings these messages, this sense of revelation?" the human asked.

The soul replied, "Gabriel, or Jibril as he's known in Islam, isn't simply a messenger in the religious sense; he is the very essence of clarity. In countless traditions, Gabriel appears at pivotal moments to shift destinies, like when he brought the Quran to Muhammad, announced the birth of Jesus to Mary, and brought visions to Daniel. These weren't just messages—they were revelations, guidance that brought people closer to their true paths. Gabriel's energy is that inner clarity that shines through when your mind is quiet, revealing insights that guide you forward."

The human considered this, finding comfort in the idea that Gabriel's energy could be as near as a whisper, as personal as intuition. "So, Gabriel is like the voice within that knows what I need, even if I resist it?"

"Exactly," said the soul. "When life feels clouded, Gabriel's presence is that inner light, guiding you back to your purpose. He's that voice urging you to listen to the truths within you, to trust that deep intuition even when logic says otherwise."

Feeling a sense of peace, the human thought about times in their life when clarity had emerged suddenly, as if out of nowhere, and realized Gabriel's presence may have been closer than they had ever known. Then, sensing the need to shift, the soul spoke of Michael.

"If Gabriel is the messenger, Michael is the protector," the soul continued. "His name means 'Who is like God,' and he's seen as a powerful force standing between light and darkness. Michael's energy is the strength that holds you steady, the courage to face what's difficult—both within and around you."

The human thought about this, remembering the stories of Michael as a warrior, a fierce guardian in times of struggle. "He's the one who fights evil, right?"

"In a way," the soul replied, "but it's not only about battling external evils. Michael's energy is also the power to face your inner shadows. He embodies the strength that rises up when life gets hard, the resolve that helps you hold onto your values even when they're tested. His presence reminds you that resilience lives within you, that you have the courage to confront even the most daunting challenges."

As the soul spoke, the human felt an inner stirring, recalling times when they had found unexpected courage in difficult situations. It was comforting to imagine that this strength had always been within, ready to emerge when needed.

"So, whenever I need guidance or courage, I can call on both Gabriel and Michael?" they asked.

"Precisely," the soul said. "Gabriel lives in the quiet certainty of your intuition, while Michael is the strength you find in moments of adversity. You might think of them as distant, but they are both parts of you—qualities you can connect with anytime. They are energies woven into your soul, accessible whenever you need them."

The human leaned back, feeling the profound simplicity of it all. Gabriel and Michael were no longer distant archetypes to be admired from afar but parts of their own spirit, qualities they could call upon, energies they had felt without realizing.

"So they're not just separate beings?" the human asked.

"No," the soul replied, "they reflect aspects of divine support that reside within every soul. When you seek guidance, Gabriel's energy is there, waiting to help you listen deeply. When you face hardship, Michael's courage is yours, helping you stand firm."

In that quiet moment, the human realized that they had never been alone in their journey. Gabriel and Michael had been there all along—energies living within, guiding and supporting them. And in that understanding, they felt a deep sense of connection to something larger, a reminder that they were always walking this path in the company of the divine.

CHAPTER: CELESTIAL HARMONY: THE SOUL'S SACRED UNION WITH ANGELS

The human leaned forward, eager to learn more about their soul's journey. A question lingered in the air—how does the soul come to seek and discover, and what role do these angelic guides play in that process?

The soul began with a story, sharing, "Imagine a young artist, lost in a haze of doubt and self-criticism. For years, they struggled, feeling as if their creativity had run dry. But one night, during a quiet moment of reflection, they had a vivid dream of a radiant figure, an angelic presence filled with warmth and light. This figure didn't speak but simply placed a hand on the artist's shoulder, filling them with peace and encouragement. When they awoke, they felt a spark, a renewed sense of purpose, even though the angel had given no specific instruction. That moment reminded them of their inner light and potential, reigniting their passion for art."

The human listened closely, absorbing the story's depth. "So, angels don't just protect us; they guide us, helping us find meaning along the way?"

"Exactly," replied the soul. "The soul is always drawn toward growth and understanding, and angels guide this search. They're there during pivotal moments, helping to reveal the truth within when the soul feels lost or uncertain."

The human reflected, realizing how some of their most transformative moments felt as if they had come from beyond, like gentle nudges toward a greater purpose. "Looking back, some of the biggest shifts in my life felt like they were... guided somehow."

The soul nodded, continuing, "That's the angelic influence. When you reach a crossroads or face a spiritual crisis, angels often appear as guides, awakening a deeper understanding within. They act like divine beacons, drawing you closer to your soul's purpose and revealing a way forward."

A memory stirred within the human, of times when a sudden insight or sense of purpose had emerged, illuminating a path they hadn't noticed before. "Can you give another example? I want to understand how angels guide us, especially during big transformations."

The soul shared, "Take the prophet Elijah, who encountered an angel in a moment of deep despair. Exhausted, he lay down under a tree, ready to give up. An angel appeared, offering food and water, not just sustaining him physically, but spiritually. It wasn't the answers he needed—only the strength to keep going, to continue his journey."

"It's like the angel reminded him his journey wasn't over," the human said thoughtfully, "that he still had a purpose to fulfill."

"Exactly," replied the soul. "Guidance doesn't always come with clear answers but can simply offer the support needed to keep seeking. Sometimes, that's all it takes—to feel supported so you can find answers within yourself."

The human reflected, recalling times they'd felt an unseen support during moments of near defeat, as if something had helped lift them back up. Then the soul spoke of more recent moments of guidance.

"During the 9/11 attacks," it shared, "many survivors reported feeling an inexplicable presence guiding them out of the collapsing buildings. One such story is of Stanley Praimnath, who was trapped on the 81st floor of the South Tower. He felt he had no hope, when suddenly a man named Brian Clark appeared, seemingly out of nowhere, calling out for anyone who might be trapped. Praimnath felt a force guiding him toward Clark, who helped pull him from the rubble, and together, they navigated their way down the tower. Praimnath has since expressed that this meeting felt divinely orchestrated, a miraculous intervention. He saw Clark as a sort of angelic presence, sent to support him during a time of unimaginable crisis."

The human paused, thinking deeply. "Even if there wasn't a literal angel in that situation, many who've faced extreme crises talk about feeling a presence or an overwhelming guidance they can't quite explain—a force helping them through impossible odds."

"Yes," replied the soul. "Angels appear when the soul is on the cusp of change, guiding it through challenges that reveal a deeper truth. When you wrestle with doubt, when you face questions of purpose, that's when angelic guidance becomes most alive. They guide you—not by giving easy answers, but by helping you discover your own strength."

A pattern began to emerge for the human, realizing these angelic figures didn't provide direct solutions but served as catalysts for inner discovery.

"It sounds like the soul's journey is as much about struggle and growth as it is about finding peace or purpose," the human reflected. "And angels... they're like companions on that journey, helping us see what we're capable of."

The soul agreed, "The soul's path isn't always clear; it winds and challenges, asking for courage. Angels illuminate the way in ways you may not even recognize, embodying qualities like strength, compassion, and wisdom—qualities you're meant to find within yourself."

The human nodded, beginning to understand. "So our struggles aren't just obstacles; they're also opportunities to grow, to connect with our purpose."

"Exactly," said the soul. "When the soul encounters an angel, it's as though the universe is gently reminding you there is purpose in the struggle and a reason to keep seeking. Angels appear to guide the soul in times of need, nudging it toward transformation and helping it grow into a truer version of itself."

The conversation deepened, and the human sensed that their journey was indeed sacred. They felt a quiet awe, realizing that angels weren't just protectors—they were guides helping unlock the potential within.

"It's humbling to think there might be a greater design," the human said quietly, "that angels could be guiding us all along, even in moments when we feel lost."

"Yes," replied the soul gently. "They remind us that our journey is worth discovering. Each encounter and each challenge offers an invitation to see ourselves more clearly and to understand that the desire to grow is itself divine. Angels are guides, yes, but ultimately, it's you—the seeker—who finds the truth."

In the quiet that followed, the human felt a deep respect for the journey they were on. Even in moments of darkness, they understood that they were not alone. The soul, like the angel, was both a seeker and a guide, helping to light the path toward self-discovery. And they realized that each step forward was, in its own way, a sacred act.

CHAPTER: TRINITY OF ESSENCE: EXPLORING THE THREE TYPES OF SOULS

The scene shifts, this time to a small, warm café, where the soul and the human sit across from each other, sipping from steaming cups, surrounded by shelves filled with books and curiosities from around the world. The soul spoke first, leaning forward as if unveiling a secret.

"You know," the soul said, a glimmer in its eye, "I think it's time you understood something deeper about yourself and others. Let's explore the three types of souls. Imagine that each of us—each soul—has a unique purpose, a reason for existing. Some souls are Seekers, others are Guardians, and some are Luminaries."

The human's eyes lit up, intrigued. "Tell me more," they said, leaning in with a smile.

The soul took a thoughtful sip of tea, letting the words brew in their mind before beginning.

"Seekers," the soul began, "are born from the raw energy of curiosity, that endless drive to explore and understand. Picture the universe as an immense library, and Seekers are the ones forever pulling new books off the shelves, diving into each one with a relentless hunger to learn."

The human chuckled. "That sounds familiar. So, Seekers are like cosmic explorers?"

"Exactly," the soul nodded, smiling. "They're the philosophers, the scientists, the artists, the wanderers. Their purpose is to push boundaries and ask questions that haven't even been conceived yet. They dive into mysteries not to find an endpoint, but to keep growing. By accumulating knowledge and experiences, they drive the evolution of consciousness itself."

"So, by seeking and learning, they're expanding the universe's understanding of itself?" the human asked, leaning in.

"Yes, exactly. Their very existence serves to expand what's known, bringing new insights and discoveries into the world. Every experience, every insight, adds a stitch to the cosmic tapestry," the soul replied. "It's their insatiable curiosity that drives not only their own growth but also the growth of all existence."

The human nodded slowly, absorbing the idea. "That sounds like a powerful purpose. But what about those who aren't Seekers? What if their purpose lies in something else?"

The soul's gaze softened, and a feeling of calm settled between them. "Then we come to the Guardians. Guardians are born from the very heart of the cosmic order. Imagine a celestial council, a gathering of souls chosen to keep harmony in the universe. Guardians are protectors and keepers of balance."

"They're like the stars holding the galaxies together, making sure everything stays in place?" the human suggested.

The soul nodded. "Yes, they're the steady, watchful stars. Guardians don't just seek knowledge; they hold the space for knowledge and life to flourish. When chaos threatens to tip the balance or when energies swing too far toward destruction, the Guardians step in. They're the stabilizers, the ones who restore harmony and bring healing."

"So, they incarnate as healers, leaders, protectors?" the human asked, sensing the gravity of the Guardians' role.

"Precisely," the soul responded. "Guardians often take roles that allow them to protect communities, safeguard the environment, or bring peace in times of conflict. They are the defenders of balance. Think of them as the ones who uphold the boundaries, allowing creation to unfold within a harmonious framework."

The human smiled, a sense of admiration shining in their eyes. "Their purpose is profound. They create the stability needed for others to grow. Without them, the universe would lose its rhythm."

The soul took a long, deep breath, a serene energy radiating from them. "And then, there are the Luminaries. They're born from the purest essence of light and love. Think of them as beams of sunlight breaking through the clouds, illuminating everything they touch. While the Seekers and Guardians work with knowledge and balance, the Luminaries inspire."

The human felt a sense of awe. "So, they're like teachers or guides who bring light to the darkness?"

"Yes," the soul replied. "Luminaries embody wisdom and compassion. Their role is to inspire, uplift, and guide. Often, they incarnate as spiritual teachers, visionaries, and healers, offering wisdom that transcends mere understanding. They remind others of their divine nature, the infinite potential within each soul. Through their presence, they awaken others, helping them see beyond illusions of separation and fear."

"Luminaries are like mirrors, reflecting back the truth of who we are," the human murmured, touched.

The soul nodded. "Indeed. They are the catalysts for spiritual awakening, helping souls to remember their own light. Where Seekers expand knowledge and Guardians preserve harmony, Luminaries elevate consciousness, guiding others toward unity and enlightenment."

The human's eyes lit up with understanding. "So, each soul has a role—Seekers push the boundaries of knowledge, Guardians hold everything together, and Luminaries lift us up to a higher understanding. Together, they create a balanced universe."

"Exactly," the soul affirmed. "This interplay between Seekers, Guardians, and Luminaries creates a dynamic, ever-evolving cosmos. They each contribute uniquely to the cosmic journey, all working toward a shared goal: the expansion and enrichment of consciousness."

The human smiled, feeling a deep sense of connection to this universal order. "So, we're all interconnected, each of us playing our part in the cosmic symphony."

The soul nodded, its presence filling the room with warmth. "Yes. And as you walk your path, whether as a Seeker, Guardian, or Luminary, remember that you are part of something much larger. Every choice, every experience, and every act of love or understanding contributes to the grand design."

They both sat in silence for a moment, letting the weight of the realization settle in.

CHAPTER: SOUL SIGNATURES: ARCHETYPES OF THE THREE ETERNAL ESSENCES

Under the soft glow of the campfire, the soul began another story, weaving archetypes into the grand design of Seekers, Guardians, and Luminaries. "Every soul has a purpose, but our roles are like colors on a vast palette," the soul said. "Some of us embody knowledge, some strength, others empathy or creation. These roles are what we call the archetypes, each one bringing a distinct energy to the universe."

The human leaned forward, listening closely as the soul continued. "Each soul type—the Seekers, Guardians, and Luminaries—finds its unique expression in one of seven archetypes: the Scholar, the Warrior, the Sage, the Priest, the Artisan, the Server, and the King. Let's walk through each one, and I'll show you how these archetypes fit within the soul types we've already explored."

The soul paused, beginning with The Scholar. "Scholars are Seekers at heart, insatiable in their quest for understanding. They're the ones who dive deeply into the mysteries of existence, driven by a boundless thirst for knowledge. Imagine a Seeker incarnating as a Scholar—someone who becomes a philosopher, scientist, or historian, endlessly drawn to the uncharted and the unknown. Scholars gather, synthesize, and share knowledge, contributing to the collective wisdom that fuels innovation and progress. Their purpose is to feed the mind and spirit, guiding others to discover new perspectives on life and the universe."

The soul smiled, its gaze shifting, and spoke next of The Warrior. "Warriors embody the Guardian spirit, with strength and resilience that protect and preserve balance. These are the souls who step forward in times of need, drawn to causes that require courage and integrity. A Guardian who takes on the Warrior archetype may become a leader in their community or a protector of those who can't defend themselves. Warriors are here to ensure that justice prevails, inspiring others to act with honor and face life's challenges with fortitude. They are the defenders of truth and harmony."

The soul's voice softened as it described The Sage. "Sages are Luminaries who carry the gift of insight and the power of storytelling. Imagine a Luminary whose purpose is to enlighten and inspire through their words, reminding people of life's deeper meanings. These souls possess a unique ability to communicate profound truths in ways that resonate with others, using humor, wisdom, and insight to guide people toward understanding. Sages remind us of the beauty and wisdom woven into every experience, helping us see the bigger picture."

After a quiet pause, the soul continued with The Priest. "Priests are the spiritual visionaries, often Luminaries connected to higher realms. These souls embody compassion and divine intuition, using their gifts to uplift and guide others on their spiritual journeys. A Priest feels called to awaken the spiritual consciousness in those around them. They are often drawn to roles where they can offer healing, a sense of purpose, and guidance, helping others connect to the divine. Imagine a Luminary Priest whose presence brings peace and clarity, someone who can bring hope to even the darkest places."

Then, with a spark of energy, the soul spoke of The Artisan. "Artisans are Seekers who thrive in creative expression. Driven by curiosity and originality, these souls see the world as an open canvas. They push the boundaries of what's possible, encouraging others to see life through a lens of wonder and beauty. A Seeker in the Artisan archetype might be an artist, a musician, or an inventor—someone who finds fulfillment in creating and transforming the ordinary into the extraordinary. Artisans show us that life is full of endless possibilities, inspiring us to explore our own creativity."

The soul's voice grew warm as it talked about The Server. "Servers are Guardians dedicated to nurturing and uplifting others, embodying compassion and selflessness. These souls are the caregivers, finding their purpose in supporting and healing those around them. A Guardian Server might become a teacher, healer, or counselor—someone who feels fulfilled by helping others thrive. Servers are the ones who create environments where people feel safe, loved, and supported. They remind us of our interconnectedness and the importance of caring for one another."

Finally, the soul spoke of The King, and there was a sense of reverence in its tone. "Kings are the natural leaders, often Luminaries whose vision and authority bring stability and progress to those they lead. Kings inspire others to come together, helping to create order and harmony in society. Imagine a Luminary King who leads with wisdom, integrity, and a commitment to the collective good. These souls take charge not for personal gain but to serve a higher purpose, helping to create a world where everyone can flourish. Kings ensure that communities stay focused, organized, and aligned with their highest potential."

The fire crackled as the soul reflected on how these archetypes intertwine with the larger roles of Seekers, Guardians, and Luminaries. "Think of it like a dance," the soul explained. "Each archetype brings its own steps and rhythm, but they all contribute to the same song—the evolution of consciousness."

The human nodded, seeing how these archetypes paint a more vivid picture of the soul's purpose. "So, each soul type—Seeker, Guardian, and Luminary—can express itself in a variety of ways, through these archetypes?"

The soul smiled, the warmth of understanding spreading between us. "Exactly. The Scholar, Warrior, Sage, Priest, Artisan, Server, and King are like facets of the same gem. Each soul brings a unique light to the universe, embodying their purpose in ways that enrich us all. Together, they create a balanced and dynamic world, where every soul's contribution is woven into the grand tapestry of existence."

In the stillness that followed, the human understood that every soul is a vital part of the cosmic symphony, each playing its role in harmony with the others. The archetypes remind us of our shared purpose and of the boundless ways we can bring our light to the world.

CHAPTER: UNIFIED ESSENCE: MERGING ARCHETYPES WITH SOUL TYPES

Sitting together in a cozy, sun-dappled café, the aroma of coffee filled the air as the two dove deeper into the wonders of soul archetypes. There was a quiet hum of conversation, but they felt like they were in their own world, trying to grasp the mystery of soul combinations and how they create such complex, rich personalities.

"So, are you saying that souls can be a mix of these archetypes?" the human asked, trying to picture it.

The soul nodded, eyes twinkling. "Exactly. Imagine each soul as an artist with a unique palette. Some souls lean more heavily into one archetype, while others blend several to express a more multifaceted purpose. Let me share some of these soul combinations with you to give you a better sense of how this works."

The human leaned in, fascinated, as the soul began with The Scholar-Sage. "Picture a soul that's both deeply curious and a natural storyteller. This is the Scholar-Sage—a powerhouse of knowledge and communication. They combine the Scholar's love of learning with the Sage's ability to captivate and convey wisdom."

"So they're like... the ultimate teachers?" the human asked, envisioning someone who lights up a classroom with both facts and stories.

"Precisely," the soul said with a smile. "Scholar-Sages exist to enlighten. They make complex ideas accessible, blending intellect with a bit of charm. Whether they're teaching, writing, or speaking, they have this gift of making people see the world in a new way."

"Alright," the human said, "I think I know someone like that. What about the next combination?"

The soul's expression shifted to something more grounded. "Let's talk about The Warrior-Guardian. This blend brings together the resilience and bravery of the Warrior with the nurturing and stabilizing energy of the Guardian."

"So, they're protectors?" the human asked, imagining someone who stands strong yet watches over others with care.

"Yes, but more than that," the soul explained. "A Warrior-Guardian feels a deep sense of duty and compassion. They're strategic, courageous, but also deeply caring. They'll step up in times of crisis, not just to lead but to make sure everyone is safe. In their communities, they're seen as pillars, grounding everyone around them with both strength and empathy."

The human felt a warmth in their chest, picturing this soul in action. "I love that balance. What's next?"

"Ah." The soul's eyes brightened. "Then there's The Priest-Artisan. Imagine a soul with a deep connection to the divine, but also a boundless creative spirit."

The human raised their eyebrows. "So, they're kind of like... visionary artists?"

"Exactly," the soul nodded. "A Priest-Artisan is someone who brings beauty and spirituality into harmony. They might create music, art, or writing that feels like a direct line to something higher. Their creations inspire spiritual awakening in others, helping people connect to higher truths through beauty and creativity."

"So, they'd be the type to create art that feels like it has a soul of its own?"

The soul smiled. "You've got it. Their work often feels imbued with a deeper purpose. It's not just art—it's a call to see beyond the surface of things."

The human took a sip of coffee, contemplating. "What about souls who feel a deep need to lead, but also to serve?"

The soul chuckled softly. "You must be sensing The Server-King. This is a compassionate leader—a mix of the caring Server with the authoritative presence of the King."

"Like someone who leads but also makes sure everyone feels valued?" the human asked.

"Exactly. The Server-King leads with empathy, building communities and organizations where well-being is the priority. They inspire loyalty because they genuinely care, not just about results, but about every individual. Their leadership is grounded in a desire to uplift others, fostering a sense of belonging."

"That sounds like someone who could run a family, a team, or even a nation," the human said, feeling the warmth of that combination. "What other blends are there?"

The soul leaned forward. "How about The Scholar-Warrior? A bit like a blend of the mind and the muscle."

"Scholar-Warrior?" the human asked, intrigued. "What does that look like?"

"This is a soul that combines the analytical mind of a Scholar with the strength of a Warrior. They're the strategists, the thinkers who are also willing to fight for truth and justice," the soul explained. "A Scholar-Warrior might be a scientist with a fierce moral compass, or a leader who uses knowledge to guide and protect. They're incredibly practical and driven to put knowledge into action."

"So they're the type to actually do something with their knowledge?"

"Absolutely," the soul replied. "They balance thought and action, using their intellect to guide their bravery and their bravery to bring their ideas to life."

The human nodded, seeing how practical yet powerful this combination could be. "Are there other combinations that blend wisdom with spirituality?"

The soul's eyes softened. "Yes, The Sage-Priest is exactly that—a soul that's both a storyteller and a spiritual guide."

"Like someone who teaches spiritual truths through stories?" the human asked, leaning in.

"Perfectly put," the soul said. "A Sage-Priest combines the charisma of the Sage with the compassion of the Priest. They have this way of making spiritual truths feel relatable and inspiring. Their words carry weight, guiding others to enlightenment with both insight and presence."

"I can picture that," the human said, nodding. "That's a powerful combo."

The soul's face lit up with excitement. "One more: The Artisan-King. This is a creative leader who combines the originality of an Artisan with the vision and authority of the King."

"Wow," the human said, smiling. "So, they're leading with creativity?"

"Exactly," the soul said. "An Artisan-King uses creativity to inspire and innovate. Their leadership encourages others to think outside the box, fostering spaces where new ideas flourish. They're the type to lead with passion and innovation, often leaving behind legacies of beauty and originality."

The human took a deep breath, trying to take in the layers and richness of each combination. "So each combo, then, brings something unique to the world?"

The soul nodded with a gentle smile. "Yes, each one adds its own richness to the cosmic tapestry. The Scholar-Sage enlightens; the Warrior-Guardian protects; the Priest-Artisan inspires. Each blend creates a synergy, a balance of strengths and wisdom, allowing each soul to express itself in profoundly unique ways. Together, these combinations add depth to existence, showing us that no two souls are quite alike."

"And yet... all of them contribute to the same greater whole?"

"Yes," the soul whispered, as if sharing a cherished truth. "Each combination is like a different color in the cosmic painting. They all have a role, a purpose, and a beauty of their own. The universe weaves every one of these threads into the endless story of existence."

The air felt charged with understanding, and the human felt the depth of every soul, every archetype, as an essential part of the cosmic dance. They sat quietly, letting the richness of these combinations settle, knowing that each blend, each soul, plays its part in the grand tapestry.

STORY: THE ETERNAL DANCE OF THE SOUL

It was a foggy evening in the old town of Inverness, Scotland. The kind of fog that rolls in thick, muffling the world and making every sound eerie. Dr. Eleanor Blackwood, a renowned historian with a penchant for the supernatural, had just received a curious letter—one that would soon unravel the mystery of her life.

The letter was written in an elegant, flowing script and bore no return address. It simply read:

"Meet me at the ruins of Dunrobin Castle at midnight. We have met before, and we shall meet again. Yours eternally, A.L."

Eleanor's curiosity was piqued. The name A.L. stirred something deep within her, a sense of déjà vu that she couldn't quite place. She had spent her career studying ancient texts and artifacts, but this felt personal, like an echo from another life.

At the stroke of midnight, Eleanor arrived at Dunrobin Castle. The ruins stood silent and imposing against the moonlit sky. As she walked through the crumbling archways, she noticed a figure standing near the old well—tall, with an air of familiarity.

"Dr. Blackwood, thank you for coming," the man said, his voice carrying a warmth that felt oddly comforting. "I am Alexander Lockwood, but you may call me Aidan."

Eleanor's heart skipped a beat. Alexander Lockwood—A.L.—the name from the letter. But why did he seem so familiar? As if reading her thoughts, Aidan smiled.

"We have known each other for centuries, Eleanor," he said. "We are part of a soul group, intertwined through lifetimes, each meeting bringing us closer to understanding and enlightenment."

Eleanor felt a rush of memories flood her mind—visions of past lives, of different eras and places where she and Aidan had crossed paths. She saw them as lovers in ancient Egypt, as comrades during the Renaissance, and as rivals in Victorian England. Each life, a different dance, but always with the same partner.

"But why now? Why meet again?" Eleanor asked, her voice trembling with a mix of excitement and apprehension.

Aidan's eyes softened. "There is unfinished business, Eleanor. In each life, we left something unresolved. This lifetime is our chance to bring closure and learn the final lessons we need to evolve."

He handed her a small, leather-bound journal. "This contains our history—our shared past. But it also holds the key to our future."

Eleanor opened the journal, her fingers tracing the ancient pages filled with entries in various scripts, each detailing their encounters through the ages. The last entry was written in a modern hand, describing their current lives and the mystery they needed to solve.

"The clockmaker," Aidan said. "We need to find him. He holds the secret to our karma and the reason we keep meeting."

The journal led them to a quaint shop on the edge of town, "Time's Keeper," run by an enigmatic clockmaker named Mr. Thorne. As they entered, the air filled with the sound of ticking clocks, each one seemingly echoing the rhythm of eternity.

Mr. Thorne, an elderly man with piercing blue eyes, greeted them as if he had been expecting them. "Ah, the eternal dancers," he said with a knowing smile. "I've been waiting for you."

He led them to the back of the shop, where an ancient, ornate clock stood. "This clock," Mr. Thorne explained, "was crafted by a master horologist centuries ago. It was designed to track the cycles of reincarnation. Your souls are bound to it."

Eleanor and Aidan exchanged a look of realization. The clock was not just a timepiece but a mystical artifact that held the key to their repeated encounters. Mr. Thorne wound the clock, and as it began to chime, the air around them shimmered.

"Each chime represents a lifetime," Mr. Thorne said. "To break the cycle, you must resolve the karmic ties that bind you. Each chime holds a lesson from your past lives that you must understand and integrate."

As the clock chimed, visions of their past lives played before them—moments of love, betrayal, forgiveness, and growth. They saw themselves making choices that led to their current lives, each decision weaving their souls closer together.

In the final chime, they saw the lesson they had missed: acceptance. Acceptance of each other, of their journey, and of the lessons learned. Tears streamed down Eleanor's face as she turned to Aidan. "I understand now. We needed to accept our past to move forward."

Aidan nodded, his eyes reflecting the same realization. "Our souls chose this dance to learn and grow together. It's time to accept our journey and embrace the future."

With that acceptance, the clock's ticking slowed, and the shimmering air stilled. Mr. Thorne smiled. "You've done it. The cycle is complete. Your souls are free to evolve."

Eleanor and Aidan felt a profound sense of peace and clarity. The weight of countless lifetimes lifted, replaced by a sense of unity and purpose.

As they left the shop, hand in hand, Eleanor knew their journey was far from over. But this time, they would face it with the wisdom of their shared past and the promise of a future unbound by time.

And so, the mystery of their eternal dance was not just a tale of reincarnation, but a testament to the enduring power of soul connections. Each lifetime a step, each lesson a rhythm, leading them towards a higher understanding and deeper love, beyond the confines of time and space

CHAPTER: TRIAD OF LIGHT: EXPLORING ANGELTYPES

The café setting lingers, the soft light casting a gentle glow as the soul and the human, feeling a sense of wonder, leaned in closer. The soul is quiet for a moment, then smiles with a knowing look, sensing the Seeker's unspoken question.

"You're wondering about the connections between these souls and the realm of angels, aren't you?" the soul asked, a spark of warmth in their gaze.

The human nodded, curiosity kindled. "Yes, I feel there must be a deeper link. Are there different types of angels, like there are types of souls?"

The soul took a deep breath and began, their voice calm yet filled with reverence. "Yes. Angels, much like souls, come in various forms, each with its own unique purpose and origin. In fact, just as the universe has Seekers, Guardians, and Luminaries, there are three distinct types of angels that align with these roles. There are the Angelic or Realm Angels, the Interplanetary Angels, and the Earth Angels. Each type aligns with the same cosmic balance of discovery, protection, and illumination."

"These angels," the soul began, "are known as Angelic or Realm Angels, and they mirror the Seekers of the soul realm. They are messengers and explorers of divine truth, roaming through the higher realms, bringing knowledge and revelation down to the cosmos."

The human eyes widened with recognition. "So, they're like cosmic guides, seeking out divine wisdom?"

"Exactly," the soul replied with a nod. "They travel across vast dimensions and realms, gathering wisdom and sharing it with other beings. These angels often appear in visions and epiphanies, guiding us with messages that help us understand higher truths. They serve as conduits for divine knowledge, much like Seekers who endlessly pursue wisdom and understanding. Just as Seekers live many lifetimes, absorbing and sharing, Realm Angels move across different dimensions to uplift the consciousness of all beings."

The human leaned back, contemplating. "So, every time we feel a sudden insight or understanding, that could be the influence of a Realm Angel?"

"Yes," the soul affirmed, "it's often their guidance that touches our minds, especially in moments of revelation. They inspire us to search, learn, and grow."

The soul's gaze shifted, a sense of protection emanating from them. "Then, there are the Interplanetary Angels. These angels are much like the Guardians among souls. Their essence is rooted in balance and preservation, safeguarding the harmony of the cosmos and its planets."

The human felt a sense of awe. "So, they're like protectors of the planets and the larger cosmic order?"

The soul nodded. "Yes. Interplanetary Angels have vast responsibilities, often acting as stabilizers for entire planets, ecosystems, and civilizations. They ensure that each realm follows its natural order, stepping in when cosmic equilibrium is disrupted. Much like Guardians, these angels protect the sacred balance, often working behind the scenes to keep harmony intact."

"So, they're like the pillars that keep everything in place," the human said, understanding deepening.

"Exactly," the soul replied, voice soft with reverence. "They are devoted to preserving the cosmic balance. Just as Guardians protect life on Earth, Interplanetary Angels protect the balance across planets and galaxies, making sure all beings have the space to grow and evolve."

The human shifted, sensing a new energy as the soul's face brightened, a soft radiance in their voice. "Finally, there are the Earth Angels, the closest counterparts to the Luminaries among souls. These angels are beings of pure love and compassion, guiding humanity and all living things toward unity and enlightenment."

The human smiled, touched. "So, Earth Angels are like beacons of light for us here?"

The soul nodded. "Yes. Earth Angels bring healing, inspiration, and awakening, often incarnating among us to help guide others toward their highest potential. They remind us of our divine nature, encouraging us to live with love and compassion. Much like the Luminaries who spread light and wisdom, Earth Angels work to uplift souls, helping them see the beauty of unity and divine connection."

"So, Earth Angels are the ones who guide us through spiritual challenges and remind us of who we are," the human said, a sense of peace settling in.

"Yes," the soul agreed, their voice gentle. "Their presence is a gift, calling us to rise above fear and live from a place of love. Earth Angels are the catalysts for transformation, showing us the path to awakening."

The human leaned back, marveling at the pattern unfolding before them. "So, each type of soul and each type of angel has a parallel, each contributing in its own way to the cosmic balance?"

"Yes," the soul replied, warmth in their smile. "Each type of soul—Seekers, Guardians, Luminaries—and each angel—Realm, Interplanetary, Earth—plays a role in the grand design. Together, they create a balanced universe, where discovery, harmony, and enlightenment move in perfect synergy. Just as souls journey through lives to grow, angels guide and support that journey."

The human took a deep breath, a sense of purpose swelling within them. "So, we are all interconnected, souls and angels alike, each with a role in this great cosmic dance."

The soul nodded, eyes shining. "Yes. Whether a Seeker, a Guardian, or a Luminary, every being, angelic or human, is woven into this intricate tapestry. Each plays a part, each contributes. And as you walk your path, remember that these angels walk with you, guiding, protecting, and inspiring. We are never alone."

They sat in silence, the café a haven of understanding, a reminder that every soul, guided by the divine hand of angels, is part of something infinitely beautiful, eternally connected, and profoundly purposeful.

CHAPTER: CELESTIAL TRIAD: A PROFOUND EXPLORATION OF THE ANGEL REALMS

The campfire crackles softly, casting a warm glow over the gathered faces, reflecting in wide, curious eyes. The soul smiled, sensing the anticipation as everyone leaned in closer, ready to dive even deeper into the mystery of the cosmos.

"Alright," the soul began, "let's start layering these realms together—the types of souls and their cosmic counterparts. Imagine the three types of souls—Seekers, Guardians, and Luminaries—finding expression not just on Earth, but also among Interplanetary and Angelic or Realm souls. Each layer adds new depth, yet they're all woven into the same universal fabric."

The soul looked around, grounding the group with an example close to home.

"Earth souls are those who embody their essence within the physical realm. Here on Earth, each type of soul finds a way to express itself in ways we encounter every day."

"Imagine the Seekers among Earth souls as the artists, philosophers, scientists, and explorers of human culture. These are the people with an insatiable curiosity, diving into ancient mysteries, unlocking the secrets of the natural world, and pushing the boundaries of human understanding. They're the ones asking big questions about life, discovering new truths, and evolving humanity's knowledge."

"Guardians on Earth step into roles as leaders, protectors, and healers. They might be conservationists, community leaders, or justice advocates. These individuals are deeply committed to the welfare of others and to maintaining harmony in society. Like an ancient oak tree with deep roots, Guardians stand steady through the storms, providing safety and stability."

"Then there are the Luminaries," the soul continued with a soft smile, "the beacons of light among us. These Earth souls might be spiritual leaders, compassionate healers, or visionary artists. They radiate hope, remind us of our potential, and elevate the world with their wisdom and compassion. They are the voices calling humanity toward unity, helping us see beyond ourselves."

The soul's gaze drifted toward the sky, drawing everyone's attention to the stars above.

"Now, let's move beyond Earth, into the vastness of the cosmos, where we find the Interplanetary souls."

"Imagine the Seekers in this realm," the soul began, "as explorers moving from planet to planet, gathering knowledge across different forms of existence. They might experience life in various environments, adapting and evolving, collecting wisdom from worlds beyond our understanding. Their journeys enrich the entire universe, connecting the different realms with insights that bind us all."

"The Guardians here are protectors on a grand scale," the soul said, voice steady. "They safeguard the balance of multiple worlds, ensuring that cosmic harmony is upheld. Think of them as intergalactic peacekeepers, helping maintain equilibrium across entire star systems. Their work supports the greater web of life, creating conditions where all beings can thrive."

"Then there are the Luminaries among Interplanetary souls, the ones who travel between worlds to share their light," the soul explained, a hint of awe in their voice. "They inspire civilizations, guiding them toward higher consciousness. Their presence serves as a reminder of unity, connecting diverse beings across the cosmos and showing them their divine potential."

The soul's voice softened, and a reverent silence fell over the group as they continued.

"Finally, we reach the Angelic or Realm souls, beings who exist beyond the physical, within the angelic and divine dimensions."

SOUL PROTECTORS

"Seekers here," the soul explained, "are celestial beings delving into divine wisdom. Their search is spiritual, exploring the nature of consciousness, divine law, and the mysteries of creation itself. These Seekers contribute to the higher understanding in the angelic realms, helping all beings grow closer to the divine."

"The Guardians in this realm are like archangels or beings of pure light, devoted to preserving cosmic balance and upholding divine order. They watch over all dimensions, offering protection and guidance to souls in need. These Guardians are the warriors of light, ensuring harmony and supporting souls across realms."

"Finally, there are the Luminaries in the angelic dimensions, the radiant beings embodying pure love and light. They serve as messengers of divine wisdom, inspiring souls throughout existence. These Luminaries illuminate the path toward enlightenment and unity, guiding others with their wisdom and reminding us of our highest potential."

The soul gazed around, catching each person's eye. "So, you see, whether they're rooted on Earth, traversing interplanetary realms, or residing in the angelic dimensions, Seekers, Guardians, and Luminaries are interconnected threads of the cosmic tapestry. Each type of soul plays a vital role: Seekers expand our understanding, Guardians preserve the delicate balance, and Luminaries uplift and guide us toward enlightenment."

As the flames flickered, casting shadows that dance along with the stars, the soul concluded, "Together, these souls and their angelic counterparts create a harmonious symphony, one that resonates with purpose, unity, and boundless potential. We are all part of this cosmic dance, each soul and angel contributing to the evolution and flourishing of life across the universe."

STORY: THE CELESTIAL CONSPIRACY

In the heart of an ancient city, nestled beside a serene lake, stood the grand library of Arcanum—a place whispered about in legends, said to house the secrets of the universe. On a crisp autumn evening, as the moon cast a silver glow over the water, a mysterious gathering took place within its hallowed halls.

Among those present were three individuals, each embodying a different soul type. Elara, a Seeker with eyes that shimmered with curiosity; Thorne, a Guardian with a steadfast gaze and an aura of calm; and Lysandra, a Luminary whose presence radiated a warm, golden light.

They had been drawn together by a shared vision—a glimpse of a celestial conspiracy threatening the balance of the cosmos. The vision revealed a powerful relic, the Orb of Eternity, which held the essence of all three soul types. If fallen into the wrong hands, it could unravel the very fabric of existence.

Elara was the first to receive the vision. In her small study, surrounded by ancient texts and artifacts, she had been poring over a manuscript when she was overcome by a vivid image. She saw the Orb of Eternity hidden within the library of Arcanum, pulsating with a luminous energy. It was a relic from a time before time, holding the potential to alter the destiny of countless souls.

Driven by her insatiable curiosity, Elara set out for Arcanum. She knew that to protect the relic, she would need allies who understood the gravity of the situation. Her search led her to Thorne and Lysandra, who had received similar visions.

Thorne, the Guardian, had been meditating in a secluded grove when the vision struck him. He saw shadows creeping towards the Orb, seeking to exploit its power for nefarious purposes. Thorne understood his role—to protect and preserve the balance. He felt the weight of responsibility settle on his shoulders, knowing that the stability of multiple realms depended on their success.

When Elara reached out to him, Thorne didn't hesitate. He knew that his skills as a protector would be crucial in safeguarding the Orb from those who sought to disrupt the harmony of the cosmos.

Lysandra, the Luminary, had been in the midst of a healing ceremony when she was enveloped by a blinding light. The vision revealed not only the Orb but also the faces of Elara and Thorne, indicating that their destinies were intertwined. As a Luminary, Lysandra's purpose was to inspire and guide, and she sensed that her light would be essential in this quest.

She joined Elara and Thorne at Arcanum, her presence bringing a sense of hope and clarity. Together, they formed a trinity, each soul type complementing the others in their mission to protect the Orb.

Inside the library, they delved into its labyrinthine corridors, guided by Elara's knowledge, Thorne's intuition, and Lysandra's illumination. They uncovered hidden passages and deciphered cryptic messages, each step bringing them closer to the heart of the mystery.

Their journey led them to a chamber deep within the library, where the Orb of Eternity rested on an ornate pedestal. Its glow was mesmerizing, casting intricate patterns on the walls. As they approached, a shadowy figure emerged from the darkness.

It was a being of immense power, a rogue Guardian who had fallen from grace. Consumed by a desire to control the Orb and reshape the cosmos to his will, he had been manipulating events to lead them here.

A fierce confrontation ensued. Thorne engaged the rogue Guardian, their clash reverberating through the chamber. Elara used her quick thinking to decipher the protective runes surrounding the Orb, while Lysandra focused her energy on shielding them from the rogue's dark attacks.

In a moment of clarity, Elara realized that the only way to neutralize the rogue Guardian was to harness the combined power of their soul types. She called out to Thorne and Lysandra, instructing them to channel their energies into the Orb.

As they did, a brilliant light filled the chamber, enveloping the rogue Guardian and dissipating his dark presence. The Orb responded to their unity, its energy stabilizing and harmonizing the chaotic forces that had been unleashed.

With the threat neutralized, the Orb of Eternity settled into a tranquil glow. The three allies understood that their mission was not just to protect the relic, but to ensure that such harmony continued across the realms.

Elara, Thorne, and Lysandra vowed to remain connected, knowing that their combined strengths were a beacon of hope for the universe. They had uncovered not just a conspiracy, but a deeper truth about the interconnectedness of all souls.

As they left the library of Arcanum, the stars above seemed to shine brighter, a testament to their triumph and the enduring power of unity.

And so, the legend of the Celestial Conspiracy became a story passed down through generations, a reminder of the Seekers, Guardians, and Luminaries who protected the delicate balance of the cosmos, ensuring that the dance of souls continued in harmony.

CHAPTER: THREADS OF ETERNITY: EXPLORING SOUL CONNECTIONS

The human leaned back in their chair, overwhelmed yet intrigued by the sheer magnitude of what they'd just heard. "Soul connections," they murmured, almost to themselves. "It's more than I thought—more than just soulmates and the romanticized version of destiny we're so often told about."

The soul's voice rose softly, steady as a tide. "Indeed, it is. Soul connections are not confined to one shape or purpose. They weave through your life in ways that challenge, support, and transform you. They are the threads that make your journey meaningful. Let's explore these threads together."

"Let's start with soulmates," the human suggested, their curiosity taking root.

"Soulmates," the soul began, "are companions on your journey. They're not always romantic, as many believe, but they always carry a deep resonance. They may come as friends, family, or partners—each one teaching you something profound."

The human thought of their best friend. "Like when I met Emily. From the moment we started talking, it was as if we'd known each other for lifetimes. She's been there for me in ways I can't even put into words."

"Exactly," the soul affirmed. "She's a soulmate. Her presence feels effortless because she understands you on a level beyond the surface. That's the beauty of a soulmate—they offer connection and growth in equal measure. But remember, not all soul connections are as gentle."

The human frowned. "You're talking about twin flames, aren't you?"

"Yes," the soul replied, its tone deepening. "A twin flame is a reflection of your own soul, split into another body. When you meet them, it's like gazing into a mirror that reveals not just your strengths, but your fears and flaws as well."

"It sounds... intense," the human said, their voice tinged with hesitation.

"It is," the soul admitted. "The purpose of a twin flame is growth, and growth isn't always comfortable. These connections can feel electrifying and magnetic, but they often come with challenges. They hold up a mirror to the parts of yourself you'd rather not face. Yet, through that friction, you find transformation."

The human was quiet for a moment, thinking of someone from their past. "There was someone once. It was like they knew me better than I knew myself, but it was tumultuous. Painful, even."

The soul's presence enveloped them gently. "That was a twin flame. Such relationships can be fleeting or lifelong, but they always leave a mark. They teach you lessons that no other connection can."

"And karmic relationships?" the human asked, a note of caution in their voice.

"Karmic connections," the soul explained, "are tied to unfinished business from past lives. They are here to teach you lessons you didn't fully learn before. These relationships can feel consuming, even draining, but their purpose is vital."

"Like breaking a cycle?" the human guessed.

"Exactly. If you find yourself repeating patterns—perhaps choosing the same type of partner who isn't good for you or facing recurring conflicts—it might be a karmic relationship at play. Once you learn the lesson, the cycle ends, and you move forward."

The human shifted in their seat, seeking a lighter topic. "What about kindred spirits? That sounds... comforting."

The soul chuckled warmly. "Kindred spirits are indeed a balm for the soul. They resonate with your values and interests. These are the friends who feel like a breath of fresh air, whose company requires no effort and no pretense."

"I've met people like that," the human said, smiling. "It's like the universe knew I needed them and just dropped them into my life."

"And you'll meet more," the soul promised. "Kindred spirits often stay with you, offering support and companionship through different phases of your life."

The human's mind wandered to a mentor they'd had in college. "What about the people who come into your life just long enough to teach you something and then leave?"

"Ah," the soul said, its voice tinged with reverence. "Those are soul teachers. They appear when you need guidance the most, often without you realizing it. They challenge your perspective, steer you onto a new path, or help you see your potential."

"Like my professor who encouraged me to take that job I was afraid of," the human mused. "It changed everything for me."

"Precisely," the soul affirmed. "Soul teachers may not stay, but their lessons endure. They are catalysts for change."

"And then there are soul companions," the human said, their tone softening.

The soul's presence seemed to glow with warmth. "Yes, soul companions are the steady ones. They are the safe harbor in life's storms, the ones who journey alongside you with unwavering support. These relationships are often lifelong, marked by mutual respect and understanding."

"They're the ones who make you feel like everything will be okay," the human said, thinking of their closest loved ones.

"Exactly. They offer stability and love that feels like home."

"And an Anam Cara?" the human asked, curious about the unfamiliar term.

"In Celtic tradition," the soul explained, "an Anam Cara is a soul friend—a connection so profound that it transcends time and space.

This is the friend with whom you can share your innermost self without fear of judgment. They see you fully and accept you completely."

The human felt a pang of longing. "That sounds rare."

"It is," the soul agreed. "But when you find your Anam Cara, it is a treasure beyond measure. They help you grow, heal, and become the best version of yourself."

The human exhaled, letting all of it settle in. "It's a lot to take in," they admitted. "But it's beautiful, too—how all these connections shape us."

"They do," the soul said gently. "Each connection is a piece of the tapestry that is your life. Some are intense, some are gentle, but all are sacred. They help you remember who you are, why you're here, and what it means to truly connect."

"And the purpose of it all?" the human asked, their voice tinged with wonder.

"The purpose," the soul said, "is love—love in all its forms. These connections remind you of your capacity to give and receive love, to grow through it, and to share it with the world. They are the threads that weave the story of your soul's journey."

The human closed their eyes, feeling the depth of the soul's words. "I'll carry this with me," they said.

"And I will carry you," the soul replied, "through every connection, every lesson, and every step of the way."

STORY: THE ENIGMA OF THE SOUL'S MIRROR

It all started on a rainy evening in Edinburgh, the kind of rain that makes the cobblestone streets glisten under the dim glow of antique lampposts. Dr. Evelyn Hart, a well-respected psychologist, was closing her clinic when she received an unexpected visitor—a man named Aidan with a peculiar request.

"A soul connection?" Evelyn echoed, raising an eyebrow as she studied Aidan's earnest face.

"Yes, Dr. Hart," Aidan replied, his voice steady but eyes revealing a hidden urgency. "I believe I have encountered someone who might be my twin flame, but... it's complicated."

Intrigued, Evelyn motioned for him to sit. "Tell me more," she said, leaning forward, her curiosity piqued.

Aidan recounted meeting a woman named Mira at a bookshop. From the moment their eyes met, he felt an inexplicable pull. It was as if he had known her all his life, yet they were strangers. Over coffee, they discovered uncanny similarities: shared childhood dreams, identical birthmarks, and even mutual memories of places they had never visited together.

"It felt like looking into a mirror," Aidan confessed. "But then she disappeared without a trace."

Evelyn's interest deepened. She had studied various types of soul connections—soulmates, twin flames, karmic ties—but Aidan's story hinted at something profoundly mystical.

"Do you have anything that belongs to her?" Evelyn asked.

Aidan handed over a small, ornate locket. "She left this behind," he said. "I hope it holds some clues."

Evelyn examined the locket, noting its intricate Celtic design. As she opened it, a tiny slip of paper fell out. Written in delicate handwriting was an address and a name: Anam Cara Cottage.

"Anam Cara," Evelyn murmured. "The Gaelic term for 'soul friend.' This might be more than just a twin flame connection. It could be an Anam Cara—someone with whom you share a deep spiritual bond."

With a renewed sense of purpose, Evelyn and Aidan set off to find Anam Cara Cottage. The journey took them through winding country roads, dense forests, and past ancient stone circles that seemed to whisper secrets of old.

When they finally arrived, the cottage was nestled in a secluded glen, surrounded by wildflowers. It felt otherworldly, as if time had forgotten this place. They knocked on the weathered wooden door, and it creaked open to reveal an elderly woman with eyes that seemed to hold the wisdom of the ages.

"I've been expecting you," she said with a knowing smile. "Come in. We have much to discuss."

Inside, the cottage was filled with the aroma of herbs and the warmth of a crackling fire. The woman introduced herself as Elara, the keeper of the Anam Cara legacy. She explained that Mira was indeed Aidan's twin flame, but their connection was part of a greater tapestry of soul bonds that transcended lifetimes.

"You see," Elara said, "your souls have been intertwined for centuries, learning and evolving together. Mira's disappearance was not a separation, but a call for you to embark on this journey. To truly understand and embrace your connection, you had to seek out your Anam Cara."

Evelyn listened intently, piecing together the intricate puzzle of Aidan's story. It wasn't just about finding Mira; it was about discovering the depth of their soul connection and the purpose it served in their spiritual evolution.

As the night wore on, Elara guided them through a series of rituals and meditations designed to open their hearts and minds to the profound bond they shared. By dawn, Aidan felt a renewed sense of clarity and connection. He understood that finding Mira was not just a physical search but a journey of the soul.

And then, just as the first light of morning filtered through the cottage windows, there she was—Mira, standing at the threshold with a serene smile.

"You found me," she said softly, her eyes meeting Aidan's with a depth of recognition that transcended words.

Evelyn watched as the two souls reunited, knowing that their journey was far from over but that they had taken the first crucial step. In that moment, she realized that the mystery of soul connections was not just about the bonds themselves but about the journey of discovery and the growth they inspired.

As Aidan and Mira embraced, Evelyn felt a profound sense of peace. The rain had stopped, and the sun now bathed the world in a golden light, symbolizing new beginnings and the endless possibilities of the soul's journey.

And so, the enigma of the soul's mirror was not merely a tale of finding a lost connection but a testament to the eternal dance of souls, ever seeking, ever growing, and forever intertwined in the tapestry of existence.

CHAPTER: ETERNAL ENCORE: WHY WE MEET THE SAME SOULS THROUGH TIME

The human sat on a sunlit bench, eyes closed, lost in thought. A gentle voice stirred within.

"Do you ever wonder why certain people feel like home the moment you meet them?" the soul asked, its tone laced with curiosity and warmth.

The human opened their eyes slowly, glancing at the blue sky above. "Yes," they replied softly. "There's this... familiarity. Like we've met before. Is that even possible?"

"More than possible," the soul replied. "It's part of our journey—an eternal encore where the same souls appear in different lifetimes, playing different roles. Let me explain."

The human leaned forward, intrigued. "I'm listening."

"Imagine life as a grand masquerade ball," the soul began, "where we change masks and costumes in each lifetime, yet the dance partners remain familiar. These partners belong to your soul group—your spiritual family."

"Soul group?" the human asked.

"Yes," the soul affirmed. "They're the ones you incarnate with across lifetimes. Bound by love, lessons, and shared growth, they help you evolve."

The human nodded slowly. "So, these are the people I feel most connected to?"

"Exactly," the soul said. "Some are here to support you, while others challenge you. Either way, they guide you toward your higher purpose."

The human tilted their head. "How do they do that?"

"By sharing lessons," the soul explained. "Think of the friend who teaches you patience, the lover who shows you the depth of unconditional love, or the adversary who forces you to grow stronger. These connections are not random—they're deeply intentional."

The soul's voice softened. "But sometimes, there's more than shared growth. Sometimes, it's about karma."

The human frowned. "Karma? Isn't that just... what goes around comes around?"

"Not quite," the soul replied with a chuckle. "Karma is about balance. It's the energy of cause and effect, yes, but it's also about learning. When something is left unresolved in one lifetime, it often carries over into the next."

The human leaned back, processing. "So, if I hurt someone in a past life...?"

"You might meet again," the soul said gently, "to heal that wound, seek forgiveness, or repay kindness. It's not about punishment—it's about growth for both souls."

The human exhaled deeply. "That's... a lot to think about."

The soul continued, "It's why you feel an instant connection or even tension with certain people. Your souls recognize the unfinished story."

"Before each life," the soul said, "we make soul contracts. We choose who we'll meet, what roles we'll play, and the lessons we'll learn together."

The human raised an eyebrow. "You're saying we plan all this?"

"Not the details," the soul clarified. "But the themes. Love, forgiveness, trust, power—each lifetime explores these in different ways. Think of the parent who teaches you responsibility or the rival who tests your integrity. These roles are agreed upon before birth."

"Even the painful ones?" the human asked hesitantly.

"Especially those," the soul replied. "Pain often holds the greatest potential for growth."

The soul paused, then asked, "Have you ever noticed how certain people reflect things back to you—your strengths, your fears, even your flaws?"

The human nodded. "Yes. It's uncomfortable sometimes."

"That's the mirror effect," the soul explained. "Familiar souls act as mirrors, showing you what needs attention or healing. A critical partner might reveal your need for self-love. A supportive friend might remind you of your own strength. These reflections help you grow."

"But it's not always easy," the human admitted.

"It's not meant to be," the soul said kindly. "Growth rarely is. But these encounters bring you closer to your true self."

"So," the human asked, "how do I know when I've met someone from my soul group?"

"You'll feel it," the soul replied. "Sometimes, it's an instant bond, like meeting an old friend. Other times, it's a deep sense of purpose in your connection—even if it's challenging."

The human smiled faintly. "Like we've danced together before."

"Exactly," the soul said. "Each encounter is a step in the dance of evolution. Whether through joy or struggle, these souls help you grow."

The soul's tone turned thoughtful. "Even ancient wisdom speaks of this. The Bhagavad Gita, for instance, teaches that the soul is eternal, moving through lifetimes to fulfill its dharma, or purpose. Psychologist Carl Jung believed in the idea of the collective unconscious—a shared pool of experiences connecting us all, much like soul groups."

The human's eyes widened. "So, science and spirituality kind of align here?"

"In ways more profound than most realize," the soul agreed. "Modern studies on near-death experiences and past-life regression also support the idea of recurring soul connections. Dr. Brian Weiss, a psychiatrist, documented cases where patients remembered past lives and recognized familiar souls across them."

The human sat quietly for a moment, then asked, "So, what should I do when I meet someone who feels... familiar?"

The soul's voice was warm. "Stay open. These connections are gifts. Learn from them, grow with them, and honor the bond. Even the challenging ones have something to teach you."

"And if I don't understand the lesson?"

"Be patient," the soul said gently. "Sometimes, clarity comes with time. Trust the process. Trust yourself."

The human exhaled, feeling a sense of peace. "This dance of souls... it's beautiful, isn't it?"

"Beyond words," the soul replied. "It's a testament to love's enduring nature—a reminder that we're all connected in this grand, eternal journey."

The human closed their eyes again, smiling. "I think I'm ready for the next step."

"And I'll be right here," the soul whispered, "every step of the way."

STORY: THE ENIGMATIC CASE OF THE UNFULFILLED SOUL CONTRACTS

"It all began on a misty autumn evening when Jane received a mysterious package at her doorstep. Inside was an old, leather-bound journal with a single, cryptic note: 'To unravel your past is to understand your present. Seek the truth within these pages.' Intrigued, Jane opened the journal, only to find it filled with intricate sketches, enigmatic symbols, and fragments of stories that seemed oddly familiar yet tantalizingly out of reach. Little did she know, she was about to embark on a journey that would unravel the mysteries of her soul contracts."

"As Jane delved deeper into the journal, she came across a name that sent a shiver down her spine: Daniel. Memories of their tumultuous relationship resurfaced, a whirlwind of passion, conflict, and unresolved tension. The journal hinted at a karmic connection, suggesting that their paths had crossed in past lives, bound by a karmic contract to resolve old grievances.

Determined to understand, Jane decided to confront Daniel, now a distant figure in her life. Their conversation was charged with emotions, revealing deep-seated issues that had plagued them both. It wasn't easy, but as they spoke, they began to untangle the threads of their shared history. Jane realized that their intense connection and frequent clashes were not random but part of a karmic cycle, a cosmic dance meant to teach them forgiveness and balance."

"Next, Jane found a sketch of a radiant heart with two interlocking circles. Beneath it was the name, Emma. Emma had been Jane's best friend since childhood, their bond unbreakable despite the passage of time. The journal spoke of soulmate contracts, agreements made to support and uplift each other through life's challenges.

SOUL PROTECTORS

Reflecting on their friendship, Jane saw the truth in this. Emma had always been her anchor, providing unconditional love and support. But the journal hinted at more – it suggested that their bond was meant to help Jane find her true self. Inspired, Jane reached out to Emma, and together, they explored deeper aspects of their connection, discovering hidden talents and passions that had been dormant for years. Their friendship took on a new dimension, enriching both their lives."

"Among the pages, Jane found a symbol of flames entwined, accompanied by the name, Alex. The intensity of her relationship with Alex had always baffled her. Their connection was magnetic, but fraught with turbulence. The journal revealed that they were twin flames, two halves of the same soul on a journey towards unity.

Determined to understand this enigmatic bond, Jane sought out Alex. Their reunion was electrifying, filled with powerful emotions and transformative conversations. They faced their deepest fears and insecurities, realizing that their struggles were catalysts for profound personal growth. The journal had been right – their relationship was about more than just romance; it was about merging their souls and achieving a higher state of being."

"Turning the pages, Jane found a symbol of an open book beside the name, Professor Carter. Memories of her college days flooded back, particularly the guidance and wisdom imparted by Professor Carter. The journal suggested a teacher-student contract, a bond meant to accelerate her growth through learning.

Jane decided to reconnect with her old mentor, seeking his advice once more. Their discussion illuminated paths she had never considered, opening doors to new opportunities and perspectives. Professor Carter's teachings had always been a guiding light, and now, they took on even greater significance. Jane understood that their contract was not just about imparting knowledge, but about igniting a lifelong passion for discovery."

"Another symbol, two hands clasped, led Jane to the name, Laura. Laura had been her colleague and confidant, their relationship marked by mutual support and understanding. The journal spoke of companion contracts, agreements to provide stability and emotional support through life's ups and downs.

Jane reached out to Laura, sharing her findings. Together, they reflected on their journey, realizing how their friendship had provided a foundation of strength during challenging times. Their bond was more than just camaraderie; it was a soul contract designed to help them navigate life's storms with grace."

"The journal's next entry featured an image of a helping hand and the name, Marcus. Marcus was a community leader whom Jane admired for his dedication to service. The journal suggested a service contract, a calling to make a difference in others' lives.

Inspired, Jane joined Marcus in his efforts, volunteering her time and skills. She discovered a profound sense of fulfillment and purpose, realizing that serving others was a vital part of her soul's journey. The journal had guided her to her true calling, transforming her life in the process."

"The last pages of the journal were the most cryptic. They spoke of challenging soul contracts, the unresolved and the incomplete. Names and faces blurred together, hinting at lessons not yet learned, emotions unhealed, and growth deferred.

Jane felt a mixture of fear and determination. She knew she had to confront these challenges head-on. Guided by the journal's wisdom, she began reaching out to people she had lost touch with, facing unresolved conflicts, and embracing difficult lessons. It was a daunting task, but with each step, she felt herself growing stronger, wiser, and more at peace."

"In the end, Jane realized that the journal was more than just a collection of cryptic messages; it was a map of her soul's journey. Each soul contract, whether fulfilled or still in progress, had shaped her life in profound ways. She learned that understanding and honoring these contracts was the key to unlocking her true potential.

As she closed the journal for the last time, Jane felt a deep sense of gratitude. The mysteries of her soul contracts had led her to a greater understanding of herself and her place in the universe. And she knew that, while her journey was far from over, she was now better equipped to navigate the intricate dance of life, guided by the wisdom of her soul and the timeless agreements that bound her to those she loved."

—-

"Jane's journey, like everyone's, is a testament to the profound impact of soul contracts on our lives. Each relationship and experience is a thread in the intricate tapestry of our existence, weaving together lessons, growth, and transformation. By embracing these connections with an open heart and a curious mind, we can uncover the deeper meaning of our lives and fulfill the sacred agreements that guide our souls' evolution."

CHAPTER: THE DANCE OF AUTHENTICITY: ALIGNING ONE'S SOUL

The human sat quietly, their thoughts swirling as they turned inward. "What does it really mean to be aligned?" they asked, the question directed not outward, but to the voice within—their soul.

"It's harmony," the soul responded gently, the words rising not as a sound but as a knowing. "It's when your thoughts, actions, and emotions move in unison with your truest essence and the purpose you carry."

The human pondered this. "But how would I recognize that? I feel so... scattered sometimes, like I'm being pulled in every direction. How would I know if I'm aligned?"

"You would feel it as a deep peace," the soul said. "Even when life is chaotic, there would be a sense of rightness, as though you are moving with the current of a vast, unseen river. You would wake up each day with clarity, knowing that your choices are guided not by fear or obligation, but by truth. It's not about perfection, but about resonance—about living in a way that reflects your highest self."

The human closed their eyes, imagining such a state. "It sounds beautiful. But it also sounds... impossible sometimes. Life is so messy, and I get lost in it. How do I even start to align?"

"By listening," the soul replied. "And trusting. Your angels are here to help you. They speak in whispers, in signs, and in the quiet nudges you feel when you're still. They are always guiding you toward alignment, reminding you of your purpose."

"Angels," the human murmured. "I want to believe that, but I don't always feel them. How do I know they're really there?"

"Do you notice the moments when something unexpected happens—a person you needed to meet, a message you needed to hear, or even the way a gentle thought arises when you're at your lowest? Those are their touches. They work through synchronicities, dreams, and the quiet unfolding of life's patterns. Archangel Gabriel, for instance, often whispers to align you with your truth and purpose, while Archangel Raphael brings healing when your energy feels fractured. Each step you take toward clarity and intention, they walk with you."

The human sighed. "It sounds wonderful, but I imagine it isn't all easy, is it? What about the challenges of alignment?"

The soul's voice softened, tinged with understanding. "Alignment is beautiful, but it requires courage. As you grow into your truth, you may outgrow certain relationships or ways of being. This can feel isolating, as if you're walking a path no one else understands. The angels know this too, and they hold you close during those moments. Archangel Michael, especially, offers strength and protection when you face resistance—whether from within yourself or from others who might not understand your path."

"I've felt that before," the human admitted. "The loneliness of change. And sometimes, it feels like the more I try to live authentically, the harder life becomes."

"That's because alignment asks you to grow," the soul said. "It asks you to step out of your comfort zone, to face fears and let go of what no longer serves you. But through every challenge, you gain resilience. You feel emotions more deeply—both the joy and the pain. And with time, you come to understand that even the hardships are part of your alignment, shaping you into the person you are meant to be."

The human felt a flicker of hope. "So, it's not about being perfect or always knowing the way. It's about trusting the process and listening to those gentle whispers, isn't it?"

"Exactly," the soul replied. "And the angels will always remind you when you stray. They leave feathers in your path, a sudden warmth in your chest, or a moment of clarity when you least expect it. Living in alignment isn't a destination; it's a journey. It's a dance, and the universe is your partner."

For a moment, the human sat with that thought, a sense of quiet settling over them. They realized they weren't alone in their quest for alignment. Their soul, their angels, and the universe itself were all moving with them, guiding them step by step toward their true self.

CHAPTER: THROUGH THE DARKNESS: THE DARK NIGHT EXPLORED

As the fire flickered in the quiet room, the human gazed into the flames, lost in thought. The warmth reached out like a gentle embrace, but their voice carried the weight of introspection. "Soul," they began, "I've been thinking about those times in life when everything seems to fall apart. The moments when we're plunged into darkness so profound it feels endless. Is that what people call the 'dark night of the soul'?"

The soul stirred, its presence a steady, luminous thread in the human's heart. "Yes," it replied, its tone imbued with calm understanding. "The dark night of the soul is more than just despair. It's a sacred unraveling, a rite of passage that strips away what no longer serves you, leaving only the essence of who you are meant to become. It's not punishment—it's transformation."

The human nodded slowly, the memories of personal struggles surfacing like faint whispers in the firelight. "It feels cruel, though. Lonely. Like being abandoned."

"That loneliness," the soul said, "is the echo of shedding illusions. The false securities you clung to—roles, attachments, even beliefs—fall away in the dark night. What remains is raw, vulnerable truth. But even then, you are never truly alone."

The human tilted their head, curious. "Not alone? It feels so isolating. Who's there in that darkness, Soul? You?"

"Always me," the soul assured, its presence like a comforting hand. "But also the angels, who watch and guide you, even if their presence feels distant. Archangel Michael often lends his strength in those moments, helping you find courage to face what feels unbearable. Gabriel whispers hope when words escape you. They are with you, waiting for you to reach out."

The human smiled faintly at the thought. "Angels... Do they really intervene? Or are they just symbols we cling to when we're scared?"

The soul's light grew brighter, its warmth steady. "They are real," it said, "and deeply invested in your journey. During your darkest hours, they illuminate paths you cannot yet see. Think of the mystic St. John of the Cross, who first wrote of this dark night. Archangel Raphael guided him through his suffering, showing him how pain could become a bridge to divine union. And you, too, are guided, even when you cannot feel it."

The human stared into the fire, seeing its dance as a metaphor for the turmoil within. "Why does it have to be so painful, though? Couldn't transformation come gently?"

"Sometimes it does," the soul admitted. "But profound growth often requires upheaval. Look at the philosophers who explored these depths. Kierkegaard spoke of the 'sickness unto death,' a despair that forces one to confront their existence. Nietzsche saw it as a necessary chaos from which stars are born. They understood that darkness breaks open what light alone cannot reach."

The human reflected on this, a trace of skepticism lingering. "So, it's all about breaking me down to build me up again?"

"Not breaking," the soul clarified. "Unveiling. The dark night peels away the layers that hide your true self. Dante's journey through the inferno is a perfect metaphor. Guided by Virgil, he descended into darkness not to be destroyed but to emerge renewed. Archangel Azrael, who gently accompanies souls through transitions, often works in this way during a dark night—helping you let go of the old to embrace the new."

The human's shoulders relaxed slightly, as if the weight of understanding was more bearable than the weight of unknowing. "It sounds like a shared experience, though. Everyone talks about it as something universal. Why is that?"

"Because it is universal," the soul replied. "Every culture, every tradition, has its version. In Indigenous cultures, vision quests are designed to lead seekers into isolation and hardship, where they face their fears and reconnect with their essence. Buddha's meditation under the Bodhi tree—confronting his inner demons before enlightenment—is another expression of this journey. The dark night is woven into the fabric of human existence."

The human's lips curved into a faint smile. "So, I'm not the only one fumbling in the dark."

"Far from it," the soul said warmly. "The dark night of the soul is both intensely personal and deeply collective. Every story you've heard, every piece of art or literature that moves you, carries traces of this journey. Raskolnikov's torment in Crime and Punishment, or Dante's descent—they resonate because they echo your own trials."

"But why does it connect us so deeply?" the human asked.

"Because in that shared vulnerability," the soul explained, "you find strength. When you confront your own darkness, you recognize it in others and extend compassion. And when you emerge from the dark night, you carry a light that helps guide others. That is why the angels support this process so closely—your growth is not just for you but for the collective healing of the world."

The human sighed, but this time it was a sigh of acceptance. "It still scares me, though. Even knowing all this, it's terrifying to think of facing such darkness again."

"Fear is natural," the soul replied gently. "But remember, you have allies. Call on the angels—Michael for courage, Gabriel for hope, Raphael for healing, Azrael for transition. Trust that I am always here, carrying you through the shadows. The fire burns now, but it will give way to warmth and light. That is the promise of the dark night."

The human gazed into the flames, their heart lighter despite the gravity of the conversation. The dark night no longer seemed like an enemy but a companion on the path to something greater. In the stillness, the crackling fire seemed to echo the truth of it all: even in the depths of darkness, light waits patiently to be found.

CHAPTER: THE CRUCIBLE OF SUFFERING: PAIN'S ROLE IN TRANSFORMATION

The human began, "this journey you've taken me on—these stages of the dark night of the soul—why does it have to be so painful? I mean, I understand the need for growth, but does it always have to come at such a cost?"

The soul seemed to shimmer in the dim light, its presence more felt than seen. Its voice, though quiet, resonated deeply, like the memory of a song. "It isn't about the pain itself, but what the pain reveals. Growth demands honesty, and honesty often means facing the parts of yourself you've hidden away. Think of the dark night as a forge—a space where the heat strips away all that is not essential, leaving behind only the truth of who you are."

"But why the descent? The struggle? The abyss?" the human pressed. "Why can't transformation just be... easier?"

The soul seemed to sigh, a tender exhale filled with patience. "Transformation isn't about ease; it's about depth. Imagine a seed buried in the soil. Before it can reach the light, it must push through the darkness. Each stage—the descent, the struggle, the abyss—is a necessary part of the process. Without them, the seed remains dormant, and its potential unrealized."

The human stared into the fire, its glow dancing in their eyes. "So, what about the glimmer? That faint light that appears after so much darkness? Is that the beginning of the end, or just another illusion?"

The soul smiled gently, a warmth that wrapped around the human like a soft blanket. "The glimmer is your first connection to hope, a sign that the darkness is not eternal. It's not an illusion—it's the truth of renewal. Like the dawn breaking after the longest night, it reminds you that light is always waiting, even when you can't see it."

The human nodded slowly, letting the soul's words settle. "And the angels?" they asked, a note of wonder creeping into their voice. "Do they really play a role in all of this?"

The soul's presence seemed to brighten. "Oh, yes. Angels walk alongside you through every stage, though their presence is often subtle. In the abyss, when you feel most alone, they are there—whispering courage into your heart. In the glimmer, they guide you toward the faint light, urging you to trust the process. They are messengers of grace, appearing in moments of need, whether in the form of a kind word from a stranger, an unexpected insight, or a sense of peace that defies explanation."

The human thought back to a time of despair when a random book had fallen from a shelf, opening to the exact passage they'd needed to read. "So, those moments—like a helping hand appearing out of nowhere or a sudden feeling of comfort—that's them?"

The soul's warmth deepened. "Indeed. Angels are subtle, but their presence is unmistakable to those who listen. Even in your darkest hour, they are there, ensuring you never lose your way completely. They remind you that, no matter how alone you feel, you are held by something greater."

The human leaned closer to the fire, their voice softer now. "And when I return—after the ascent—what then? What's the point of coming back if I'll never be the same?"

"Precisely because you won't be the same," the soul said gently. "The return is not about resuming life as it was. It's about living as you are now—transformed, authentic, and whole. The scars you carry are proof of your journey, and they hold the wisdom you've earned. By returning, you bring light into the world, not only for yourself but for others still wandering in the dark. You show them that the night ends, and the dawn is worth waiting for."

For a long time, the human was silent, the firelight reflecting the flicker of something new in their eyes—hope, perhaps, or resolve. "So, it's not just about me," they said finally. "It's about what I bring back to others, too."

The soul's presence swelled, like the glow of the fire reaching every corner of the room. "Exactly. The journey of the dark night transforms you, but its gifts are meant to be shared. Every step, every struggle, every glimmer of light you've found—they ripple outward, touching the lives of those around you. This is how the world heals, one soul at a time."

And as the human gazed into the dancing flames, they felt a deep sense of connection—to the firelight, to the soul, to the angels unseen but present, and to a world that, even in its darkness, held infinite light waiting to be revealed.

CHAPTER: TRIUMPH OVER THE DARK NIGHT

The fire crackled softly between them, its warmth cutting through the cool stillness of the night. The human leaned back, their thoughts swirling in the quiet, when the soul's voice broke the silence.

"So, you've made it through the darkness," it said gently, a tone both knowing and curious.

"Barely," the human murmured, staring into the flames. "I didn't think I'd ever see the other side. The nights felt endless."

The soul seemed to smile, though its presence was more felt than seen. "That's the nature of the dark night. It feels eternal while you're in it. But tell me, what did you find there?"

The human hesitated, the memories still raw. "I found myself, I suppose. Or at least, parts of me I didn't want to see. It was like standing in front of a shattered mirror, trying to piece together who I really am."

"That's the gift of the dark night," the soul replied. "It strips away the illusions. You finally see what's real, even if it's uncomfortable at first."

The human thought about the moments of revelation—the painful truths they'd faced about their fears, their desires, their failures. "It wasn't just uncomfortable. It was terrifying. Like standing at the edge of an abyss and not knowing if I'd fall or fly."

"And yet, here you are," the soul said. "Tell me, how does the light feel now that you've emerged?"

The human closed their eyes, breathing in the stillness. "It's... clearer. Lighter, somehow. Like I've left something heavy behind, but I'm not sure what it was."

"You've shed the weight of the old self," the soul explained. "The part of you that clung to expectations, to fears that weren't truly yours.

That's the transformation. The light you feel now isn't new—it's always been there. The darkness just helped you see it more clearly."

The human opened their eyes and looked at the soul. "So, this clarity I feel... is it permanent? Or just another illusion?"

"It's neither," the soul said softly. "It's a beginning. A new way of seeing. Think of it like dawn after a long night. The light isn't static—it grows as you move forward, as you trust yourself more deeply. But tell me, what else do you see now that you couldn't before?"

The human thought for a moment, the words forming slowly. "Compassion. For myself, for others. It's like, having walked through my own darkness, I can see theirs more clearly too. And instead of judgment, I feel... connection."

The soul's warmth deepened, as though it were nodding in approval. "That's the gift you carry now. Compassion born from understanding. It's a rare kind of strength, one that has the power to heal—not just you, but others as well."

The human remembered moments where they'd felt that connection—a stranger's kind word, a friend's steady presence. "It's strange," the human admitted. "The things I once thought were small or insignificant now feel enormous. Like every little kindness is a spark in the dark."

The soul's voice was almost a whisper. "That's because you've learned to see with new eyes. The darkness has taught you to cherish the light, no matter how faint. But tell me, what will you do with this clarity, this connection you've found?"

The human stared into the fire, the flames dancing like tiny messengers. "I want to create," the human said finally. "To share what I've learned. Maybe through my writing or just... in how I live. I want others to know they're not alone in their darkness."

"That's the ultimate transformation," the soul said. "To take what you've gained and offer it to the world. It's not about grand gestures—it's in the small, authentic ways you show up. Like the angels who guided you, unseen but felt. Do you remember those moments?"

The human nodded, the memories rising unbidden. "There were times I felt completely lost, but then something would happen. A song, a book, even just a stranger's smile. It felt like... like someone was leaving breadcrumbs for me to follow."

"Angels come in many forms," the soul said. "They don't always wear wings or halos. Sometimes they're the people who cross your path at just the right moment. Sometimes they're the whispers of your own intuition. They were there, even when you couldn't see them."

The human felt a warmth in their chest, the fire reflecting in their eyes. "I want to be that for someone else," they said. "A light in the dark, even if it's just a small one."

"And you will be," the soul replied, its voice steady and sure. "The darkness didn't break you—it remade you. You've emerged with gifts you couldn't have found any other way. Now, your journey is to share those gifts, in whatever way feels true to you."

The human leaned back, the weight of the journey finally giving way to a quiet peace. The night was no longer something to fear—it had become a part of them, a teacher, a guide. And as the fire crackled softly, the human realized that the dawn wasn't just out there—it was within them, growing brighter with every breath.

STORY: THE LIGHT IN THE SHADOWS

It had been months since Elena emerged from her dark night of the soul. The bleak period had felt endless, each day a struggle against an unseen weight pressing down on her spirit. But now, as the first tendrils of dawn crept into her life, she felt an inexplicable sense of renewal. Little did she know, her journey through darkness had only just set the stage for a mystery that would challenge her newfound clarity and purpose.

One crisp autumn morning, as the sun painted the sky with hues of orange and pink, Elena received a letter. It was an unusual sight in her digital-dominated life—an old-fashioned, handwritten envelope sealed with a wax emblem. The symbol was familiar, yet she couldn't place where she had seen it before.

The letter contained a single sentence: "In the heart of the labyrinth, your true path awaits."

Intrigued and slightly unnerved, Elena decided to investigate. Her curiosity was piqued by the enigmatic message, and she felt a strange pull, as if her soul recognized a call to action.

Elena's search led her to a forgotten part of her hometown—a place she had once visited as a child but had since faded into obscurity. The labyrinth was an ancient hedge maze in the heart of an overgrown garden, shrouded in mystery and long abandoned. As she stood at its entrance, the morning mist curling around her, she felt a flicker of déjà vu, a sense that she had been here before, in another time or perhaps another life.

With each step into the labyrinth, memories of her dark night resurfaced—not as tormenting shadows, but as guiding lights. The twists and turns of the maze mirrored her own internal journey through despair and into enlightenment. She realized that the path she now walked was symbolic of her own soul's journey, each choice a reflection of her inner transformation.

Deep within the labyrinth, she found a small clearing with a stone pedestal at its center. On the pedestal lay a book bound in dark leather, the same emblem from the letter embossed on its cover. As she opened the book, she discovered it was a journal—her great-grandmother's, Eliza, the same woman who had once guided her through her dark night in dreams and visions.

Elena devoured the journal's pages, uncovering Eliza's own journey through a dark night of the soul. Eliza had faced similar trials, and her writings revealed secrets about their family's connection to the mystical and the labyrinth itself. The journal spoke of a hidden lineage of guardians, each generation tasked with protecting a powerful secret: a relic said to hold the wisdom of ages, capable of illuminating the soul's purpose.

The journal ended with a cryptic note: "The relic lies within, guarded by the soul's truest reflection."

Elena's heart raced as she pieced together the clues. The labyrinth was not just a physical maze but a symbolic journey into the self. The relic she sought was a mirror—an ancient, ornate mirror hidden within the clearing. As she wiped away the dust from its surface, she saw her reflection, not just as she was but as her truest, most enlightened self.

In that moment, she understood. The dark night of the soul had been a crucible, refining her spirit and stripping away illusions. The relic was a reminder that true wisdom and guidance come from within, from the soul's deepest truths.

Holding the mirror, Elena felt a surge of clarity and purpose. She knew that her role as a guardian was to share this wisdom, to help others navigate their own dark nights and emerge into the light. The labyrinth, the journal, and the mirror were all part of a larger tapestry, guiding her towards her destiny.

As she left the labyrinth, the sun breaking through the mist, she felt a profound sense of peace and empowerment. The mystery had not only revealed her path but also affirmed her soul's journey. She was ready to embrace her role, knowing that every shadow she encountered would only lead her closer to the light.

In the days that followed, Elena began to share her story, helping others understand their own dark nights and guiding them towards their inner light. The relic and the labyrinth became symbols of hope and transformation, testaments to the enduring strength of the human spirit.

And so, in the quiet corners of her town, amidst the whispers of old trees and the rustling leaves of the labyrinth, a new chapter began—a chapter where the light of understanding and the warmth of empathy illuminated the path for all who sought it, guided by the soul's eternal journey from darkness into light.

STORY: A DARK NIGHT OF THE SOUL: A MYSTERY UNFOLDS

Picture a small, isolated village nestled in the foothills of a towering mountain range. This village, Elmswood, is known for its thick, ancient forests and the mist that clings to the trees like a forgotten whisper. The villagers live simple lives, but there's an air of unease that hangs over them. They speak in hushed tones about the "Old Path"—a trail leading deep into the forest that no one dares to tread after dark.

One autumn evening, as the sun dipped below the horizon, a young woman named Clara ventured into the forest. Clara was known for her curious nature and her knack for uncovering secrets. She'd heard the legends of the Old Path and the dark night of the soul, a journey said to confront one's deepest fears and desires. Determined to document her findings for her blog, Clara set out with a camera, a notebook, and a flashlight.

But Clara didn't return.

The village was thrown into a state of panic. Search parties were formed, but they found no trace of Clara. Her parents, desperate and grief-stricken, reached out to an old friend, Dr. Alistair Halloway—a psychologist and an expert in the phenomenon of the dark night of the soul. Dr. Halloway had studied cases of people undergoing profound spiritual crises, often triggered by extreme experiences or deep introspection.

"I need to go there," Dr. Halloway said to Clara's parents. "I need to walk the Old Path."

Dr. Halloway arrived in Elmswood, greeted by the anxious faces of the villagers. He listened to their stories, trying to piece together the mystery. An elderly woman, Ms. Thornfield, mentioned seeing strange lights in the forest the night Clara disappeared. Another villager, Mark, claimed to have heard eerie, unearthly music drifting through the trees.

Equipped with a map of the forest, Dr. Halloway set out at dusk, determined to uncover the truth. As he walked the Old Path, the forest seemed to close in around him, the mist thickening and the shadows deepening. He felt a growing sense of dread, as if the very air was charged with unseen energy.

Hours into his journey, Dr. Halloway stumbled upon an old, decrepit cabin. The door creaked open as if inviting him inside. Within, he found Clara's notebook, her handwriting frantic and scrawled across the pages. She wrote about feeling watched, about strange symbols carved into the trees, and about a mysterious figure she glimpsed in the shadows.

Suddenly, a figure appeared at the doorway—it was Clara, but she looked different. Her eyes were wide with a mix of fear and revelation. "You shouldn't have come," she whispered. "This place... it shows you the truth, but it's a truth you might not want to see."

Clara explained that the forest wasn't just a physical place—it was a manifestation of the dark night of the soul. It forced those who entered to confront their deepest fears and unresolved traumas. Clara had faced visions of her past, her regrets, and her insecurities. She had been on the brink of despair when she found the cabin, a place of refuge where she could process her experiences.

Dr. Halloway realized that his own journey was just beginning. The forest started to change, the shadows morphing into familiar shapes—his childhood home, his long-lost friends, moments of guilt and grief he had buried deep within. He saw himself not as the composed psychologist, but as the vulnerable man he had always been.

Morning light filtered through the trees as Dr. Halloway and Clara made their way back to Elmswood. They were greeted with tears of relief and joy. Clara's parents embraced her, but they noticed the change in her—she was quieter, more contemplative, as if she had aged years in just a few days.

Dr. Halloway spoke to the villagers about the dark night of the soul, explaining that it was a journey each person had to take alone, but also a journey that could lead to profound transformation. Clara's experience had revealed secrets about herself that she never knew, but it also gave her a newfound strength and clarity.

In the weeks that followed, the village of Elmswood began to change. The Old Path was no longer feared but respected. The villagers started to see it as a place of personal pilgrimage, a path where one could confront their inner demons and emerge stronger. Dr. Halloway continued his work, now with a deeper understanding of the dark night of the soul, using his experiences to help others navigate their own inner landscapes.

CHAPTER: THE ETERNAL RETURN

The fire crackled softly, its warmth wrapping around the room like an old, comforting embrace. The human sat across from their soul, feeling the profound stillness that came when stepping beyond time and space. They had been reflecting on their life's purpose and the challenges that seemed to weave through it when a thought surfaced.

"Tell me," the human began, "about past lives. Have I lived before? And if so, what do they mean for me now?"

The soul responded with the gentle patience of eternity. "You have lived many lives, each one a chapter in the grand book of your existence. These lifetimes are threads in the tapestry of your being, and every experience, every choice, every lesson has contributed to the essence of who you are today."

The human leaned forward, intrigued. "So, I carry those experiences with me? How do they show up?"

"Sometimes as wisdom," the soul explained. "A talent that feels second nature, like the painter who picks up a brush and creates beauty with ease, or the healer who instinctively knows how to mend a broken spirit. These are gifts refined through lifetimes. But not everything is so seamless. There are also unresolved patterns—wounds left unhealed, fears left unchecked—that whisper to you even now."

The human frowned slightly. "Those fears I can't quite explain. The anxiety that seems to have no source... could those come from another life?"

The soul nodded. "Yes, and recognizing them is the first step to healing. The angels often guide you in this process. Archangel Jeremiel, for instance, helps you review the threads of your past lives during moments of reflection, especially in dreams or meditative states. When you sense a memory or emotion that doesn't feel tied to your current life, know that it may be a fragment from your past calling for resolution."

The human's heart softened at the thought. "And how do I heal those fragments?"

"By facing them with love," the soul replied. "Past life regression, meditation, and prayer can help you access these memories. But it's not just about remembering; it's about transforming. Archangel Raphael can assist in this healing, helping to release old pain and integrate those experiences into the wholeness of your being. Each wound you heal now ripples backward and forward across time."

The human's brow furrowed. "Ripples? You mean it affects not just me now but... other versions of me?"

The soul's presence seemed to expand, radiating warmth. "Indeed. Time is not as linear as you perceive it. Mike Ricksecker's stacked time theory offers a glimpse of this truth: imagine your past, present, and future as layers stacked atop one another, existing simultaneously. Your lifetimes are like pages in a book, all held together, all connected. When you heal in this moment, the energy shifts across those layers, touching your past and future selves alike."

The human felt a flicker of understanding. "So, by healing my present, I'm also healing my past lives?"

"Yes," the soul said. "And even your future ones. Imagine your lifetimes as a garden. A flower you water now sends its roots deep into the soil, nourishing the plants beside it. This is the interplay of your existence. And your angels—especially Archangel Metatron, the keeper of sacred knowledge—guide you through these layers, helping you access insights from other times to enrich your present journey."

The human let the thought settle. "It's overwhelming to think about all those lives, all those lessons. How do I make sense of it all?"

"By trusting the wisdom of your soul and the guidance of your angels," the soul reassured. "Your soul contracts act as a roadmap, created with the knowledge of your past and the potential of your future. Each life builds upon the last, contributing to your growth and evolution. Every challenge and connection is purposeful, leading you closer to your divine truth."

The human's gaze softened. "So, this life... it's not just about me now. It's part of something so much greater, isn't it?"

"Exactly," the soul replied. "You are a spark of the eternal, ever-evolving and ever-connected. When you reflect on your struggles, remember that they are part of a larger story—a story written in collaboration with the angels, with divine guidance, and with the wisdom of lifetimes."

For a moment, the room was quiet, the only sound the fire's gentle crackle. The human closed their eyes, feeling the vastness of their soul's journey and the comfort of the angels' presence. They realized that they were never truly alone. Their past, their present, and their future were interwoven, supported by an infinite web of love and purpose.

As the flames flickered, the human whispered, "Thank you," not just to their soul but to the unseen forces that had guided them through countless lifetimes. In that moment, they felt it—the timeless dance of existence, the wisdom of the ages, and the clarity of now—all held together in the embrace of eternity.

STORY: THE ECHOES OF ETERNITY

It was a quiet, moonlit night when Isabella received the package. Delivered by an unknown courier, it was an unassuming box wrapped in weathered parchment. Her heart raced with curiosity and a hint of trepidation as she unwrapped it, revealing an old, leather-bound journal and a peculiar antique key.

The journal's first page bore a simple, cryptic message: "The answers you seek lie in the shadows of your past and the light of your future. Use the key wisely."

Isabella had always been intrigued by the mysteries of the soul. Her journey through a dark night of the soul had left her with a deep sense of purpose and an unquenchable thirst for understanding. She knew this was more than just a random delivery—it was a call to a deeper

With the journal and key in hand, Isabella sought the guidance of Dr. Ellery, a renowned past life regression therapist. Under hypnosis, Isabella found herself transported to 18th-century France. She was Eléonore, a young woman deeply involved in secretive alchemical practices. Eléonore had crafted an intricate labyrinth beneath her manor, a place where she and her fellow alchemists sought to unlock the secrets of the universe.

The regression revealed a critical moment: Eléonore and her companions had hidden a powerful relic, said to connect the present to all past and future lives. But their work was left unfinished, abruptly halted by betrayal and chaos.

Dr. Ellery helped Isabella decode the fragmented memories. The antique key was the key to the labyrinth Eléonore had created. With newfound determination, Isabella traveled to France, guided by the echoes of her past life.

Upon arriving at the dilapidated manor, she found the labyrinth exactly as it had appeared in her memories. As she navigated the twisting corridors, the air thick with ancient energy, she felt a deep sense of familiarity and purpose. The key fit perfectly into a hidden lock, revealing a hidden chamber illuminated by an otherworldly glow.

In the center of the chamber lay the relic—an ornate mirror, much like the one in her great-grandmother's journal. As Isabella gazed into the mirror, she saw not just her reflection but a cascade of images from her past lives. Each face, each story, was a fragment of her soul's journey. Eléonore's face appeared, whispering words of wisdom and guiding Isabella to understand the deeper truth.

The mirror didn't just show the past; it revealed the concept of stacked time. Isabella saw herself not just in past lives, but in future ones, all existing simultaneously. She understood that her actions in the present could heal the past and shape the future, creating a ripple effect across time.

The journal had spoken of a soul contract—an agreement she had made across lifetimes to find and protect this relic, ensuring its wisdom was used for the greater good. Isabella realized her role wasn't just about her personal journey but about fulfilling a larger purpose that spanned centuries.

As Isabella left the labyrinth, the weight of her discovery settled upon her. She was part of a lineage of guardians, each tasked with preserving the relic's secrets and guiding humanity towards enlightenment. Her journey through past lives, the labyrinth, and the revelations of stacked time had equipped her with the knowledge and strength to fulfill her soul contract.

Back in her home, surrounded by the journal, the key, and the relic, Isabella felt a profound sense of peace and clarity. She knew her journey was far from over. The relic's power was not just a treasure but a tool for healing and transformation. She began sharing her story, helping others understand their own soul contracts and the timeless nature of their journeys.

Isabella's tale became a beacon of hope, illustrating the interconnectedness of past, present, and future. Her understanding of stacked time and soul contracts provided a framework for others to navigate their own spiritual paths, bridging the gaps between lifetimes and unlocking the mysteries of the soul.

As we sit here, the fire's glow reflecting in our eyes, we marvel at Isabella's journey. Her story reminds us of the profound depth of our own soul's journey. By understanding our past lives, honoring our soul contracts, and embracing the concept of stacked time, we can navigate the complexities of our existence with greater wisdom and purpose.

This mystery, unfolding across time and space, invites us to reflect on our own paths. We see how the past shapes our present, how our present actions ripple into the future, and how everything is interconnected in the grand tapestry of our soul's journey. Here's to embracing the mystery, honoring our soul's purpose, and navigating the timeless dance of existence with grace and awareness.

CHAPTER: WALK-INS AND THE ANGELIC DANCE OF THE SOUL

The fire's warmth wrapped around them as the soul continued, its voice weaving through the night, deep and calm. "Tonight, let's dive into something a bit out there but profoundly transformative—walk-ins. It's a rare phenomenon, but when it happens, angels are often nearby, guiding and supporting the souls involved. You see, sometimes a soul has traveled so far, it just... needs a break. Or maybe it's ready for a change, but the body it's in still has important work to do. That's when angels—like Michael, Gabriel, and Raphael—often step in, orchestrating a shift that lets another soul take over or join the journey."

The human looked at the soul with curiosity. "You're telling me angels... help souls swap places?"

The soul nodded. "In a way, yes. There's an entire process to it. When a soul swap happens, it's usually something planned long in advance, often with the support of archangels to make sure it's as seamless as possible. Each type of walk-in has its purpose, and the angels' roles vary based on the kind of support needed. Let me walk you through it."

"Imagine a soul who's been through deep pain, struggling to carry on—burnout, trauma, emotional wounds. That's where a Healing Walk-In can step in," the soul explains. "But it doesn't happen alone. Archangel Raphael, the angel of healing, is typically nearby, guiding this exchange to bring fresh energy and restoration to the person's spirit."

The human nodded, picturing Raphael's green light surrounding the soul in need. "So Raphael orchestrates it?"

"Yes. Raphael's presence ensures that the incoming soul arrives with a healing touch, to ease suffering and renew purpose. The person might feel a sudden sense of peace, a return of energy, or a shift in habits and perspectives. Raphael doesn't force healing, but his presence supports it, helping this walk-in bring the light and strength needed to move forward."

The soul's expression grew intense. "Now, let's say a soul has a mission—a profound purpose that it needs to accomplish but just... can't. Enter the Mission Walk-In. This is where Archangel Michael often comes in. Known for his strength and leadership, Michael facilitates the switch, clearing away doubts and fears to ensure the new soul is prepared to take on its mission."

The human imagined Michael's powerful, blue energy surrounding the exchange. "So, Michael's there to help bring in a new sense of direction?

"Exactly," the soul replied. "The Mission Walk-In doesn't happen randomly; it's often pre-arranged. With Michael's support, this soul can dive in with focus and courage. The person might experience a surge in confidence or new passions—a sudden drive to achieve something impactful. It's as if a new compass appears, guiding them with clarity."

The soul leaned in, lowering its voice. "Now we're getting into complex territory: The Karmic Walk-In. This exchange is all about balancing energies and resolving unfinished business. And for this, Archangels Zadkiel and Jophiel often step in. Zadkiel is known for mercy and transformation, while Jophiel brings wisdom and clarity. Together, they help guide the souls through this intricate exchange."

The human felt a shiver, imagining how much energy must be involved. "So what does the Karmic Walk-In actually do?"

"This walk-in is like balancing an ancient scale," the soul explained. "The original soul and the incoming soul might have unresolved karma—debts, lessons, promises left incomplete. Zadkiel's violet flame of mercy cleanses the path, while Jophiel's golden wisdom helps both souls learn what's needed to move forward. The person may suddenly find themselves focused on past relationships, personal challenges, or even new responsibilities. It's not easy, but it's transformative."

"Now, not all walk-ins are full replacements," the soul said with a smile. "Some are what we call a Soul Braid—two souls sharing the same body, each bringing their strengths and insights. This process is often overseen by Archangel Haniel, who governs harmony and inner peace, and Archangel Chamuel, who's known for relationships and empathy."

"Two souls in one body?" the human asked, trying to wrap their mind around it.

The soul nodded. "Yes, two souls blending their energies. Haniel and Chamuel help them find balance. Chamuel's pink light brings love and understanding, while Haniel's gentle influence helps them coexist harmoniously. Those with a Soul Braid often feel a blend of personalities—maybe stronger empathy or shifting interests. It's like they're living multiple perspectives, learning from both souls' unique experiences."

The soul's gaze softened. "Finally, we have the Transitional Walk-In. This occurs during times of major life transition—near-death experiences, intense trauma, or spiritual awakenings. Archangels Uriel and Metatron usually guide these exchanges. Uriel brings divine light and wisdom, helping the original soul let go and preparing the way for the new soul, while Metatron, the keeper of the Akashic records, ensures alignment with the soul's highest purpose."

"Uriel and Metatron... so they're helping make sure it's smooth?" the human asked.

"Exactly," the soul replied. "Uriel's light illuminates the path forward, helping the person feel clarity and comfort through the change. Metatron, with his connection to universal knowledge, ensures that the incoming soul's purpose aligns with the body's potential. People with a Transitional Walk-In often feel as though they've been reborn. They may sense new insights, a pull toward spirituality, or a shift in their life direction."

The soul leaned back, watching the embers glow. "Walk-ins usually occur during altered states—deep sleep, a coma, near-death, moments of trauma, or profound meditation. Angels like Gabriel, the divine messenger, and Zachariel, the angel of transformation, help facilitate these exchanges, ensuring they are smooth and guided. Gabriel's silver light often surrounds the transition, bringing a sense of peace, while Zachariel helps with the deep inner changes that follow."

The human could almost feel Gabriel's calming energy in the air. "So... no pain?"

"None at all," the soul assured. "The angels are there to make it seamless. Though people may experience identity shifts, changes in preferences, or a new sense of purpose. It's like a subtle reawakening, guided and supported."

"So what's the point?" the human asked. "Why do these walk-ins happen?"

The soul smiled knowingly. "Walk-ins are all about growth. Whether it's for healing, fulfilling a mission, resolving karma, sharing wisdom, or preparing for a transition, walk-ins are cosmic resets. They signify that the universe's plan for growth continues, even if it requires fresh energy, purpose, or perspective."

The soul's words lingered in the air, filled with the warmth of the angels who guide and guard these exchanges. Walk-ins might seem extraordinary, but they're a powerful reminder of the resilience, adaptability, and mystery of every soul's journey. Guided by angels, these souls continue on their path, interconnected and supported by an unseen realm, always expanding towards new growth and purpose.

STORY: TRANSIENT SOULS

The sun dipped below the horizon, casting long shadows across the small town of Brookwood. Detective Sam Carson leaned against his car, sipping his coffee and watching the colors of the sky deepen. He wasn't a believer in the supernatural, but the case he'd been handed was anything but ordinary.

A week ago, Julia Marks, a local teacher, had collapsed in the middle of her classroom. She was rushed to the hospital, and after a few hours, she woke up, seemingly fine. But everyone who knew her insisted that Julia was different. Her once shy and reserved demeanor had been replaced with confidence and an uncanny knowledge of things she'd never shown interest in before.

Sam had been called in when Julia's husband, Mark, reported that his wife had returned home with no memory of their life together. She didn't recognize their home, their pets, or even her own reflection in the mirror. Mark was convinced that the woman in his house wasn't Julia at all.

"So, you're telling me your wife is a completely different person?" Sam asked Mark as they sat in the Marks' living room.

"Not just different, Detective," Mark said, wringing his hands. "It's like she's been replaced. She talks about places she's never been, people she's never met, and she doesn't remember our wedding, our vacations, nothing."

Sam nodded, scribbling in his notepad. "Has she seen a doctor?"

"Yes, and they say there's nothing physically wrong with her. It's like... like someone else is in her body."

The term "walk-in" floated through Sam's mind, a phrase he'd heard from a quirky old woman who ran the town's metaphysical shop. She had once told him about souls that could switch places, walk into another's life when the original soul had had enough. At the time, he had dismissed it as nonsense.

But now?

Sam decided to visit the metaphysical shop, hoping for some insight. The shop, named "Ethereal Echoes," was a cluttered haven of crystals, incense, and ancient books. The owner, Elara, was a petite woman with silver hair and eyes that seemed to see right through him.

"Detective Carson, what brings you to my little corner of the world?" she asked with a knowing smile.

"Elara, I need to ask you about walk-ins," Sam replied, feeling a bit foolish.

"Ah, the rare phenomenon of souls switching places," she said, her eyes lighting up. "It's not common, but it does happen. Why do you ask?"

Sam explained Julia's case, and Elara listened intently, nodding occasionally.

"It sounds like a classic walk-in situation," she said. "The original soul left, and a new one took its place. The new soul retains some memories, but the essence, the personality, is different."

"Why would this happen?" Sam asked, skepticism lacing his voice.

"Various reasons," Elara replied. "The original soul might have been too weary, or there could be a higher purpose for the new soul's arrival. Sometimes, it's to complete a mission, heal past traumas, or balance karmic debts."

Sam rubbed his temples. "How can we prove this?"

"You can't, not in the conventional sense," Elara said. "But you can try to communicate with the new soul, understand its purpose."

Back at the Marks' house, Sam decided to take a different approach. He sat down with Julia, now eerily calm and composed, and asked, "Who are you?"

Julia looked at him, her eyes sharper than he remembered. "I am Julia," she said, then paused. "But not the Julia you knew. My soul... it had to leave. I've come to finish something important."

"What is it?" Sam pressed.

"I don't fully remember," she admitted. "It's like pieces of a puzzle I'm trying to put together."

Days turned into weeks, and slowly, bits of Julia's new life started to make sense. She began visiting places she'd never been, connecting with people who claimed to have seen her in their dreams. She spoke of a mission, fragments of memories that weren't hers but felt crucial.

Sam kept close tabs on her, watching as Julia pieced together her new identity. One evening, she approached him with a journal, its pages filled with intricate drawings and notes.

"I think I was brought here to protect something," she whispered, her voice trembling. "Something powerful."

Sam knew he was in deep now, far beyond the realm of logic and reason. But as he looked into Julia's determined eyes, he realized this was no longer just about solving a mystery. It was about understanding the unseen threads that connect all lives, the purpose hidden in the inexplicable.

Together, they delved into Julia's newfound mission, uncovering secrets that had been buried for lifetimes. And as they navigated this strange journey, Sam began to see that sometimes, the most extraordinary mysteries lie not in the evidence we can see, but in the souls we cannot

CHAPTER: SOUL WISDOM

The human sat cross-legged, their hands resting lightly on their knees, eyes closed in quiet reflection. "I feel like I know things... things I've never been taught, never read or heard. Where does that come from?"

The soul's voice responded softly, like a warm wind brushing through the leaves. "That is your soul wisdom, the deep knowing your essence carries across lifetimes. It's not about facts or books but the truths etched into your being from all the lives you've lived."

The human opened their eyes slowly. "All the lives I've lived? You mean this isn't the first?"

"No," the soul said with a gentle laugh. "You've been here before, and you will be here again. Every life is a chapter, every experience a lesson. Together, they form a vast, intricate story—one that shapes your understanding of existence, love, and connection. That is the gift of soul wisdom."

The human furrowed their brow. "So it's like... a collection of memories?"

"In a way," the soul explained, "but not memories as you know them. Soul wisdom is deeper. It's the empathy that allows you to feel another's pain as if it were your own. It's the serenity you find in chaos because you know, deep down, that everything is as it should be. It's the strength to forgive because you've learned that holding on only binds you."

The human nodded, a flicker of recognition crossing their face. "But how does this wisdom grow? What teaches it?"

"Life itself," the soul answered. "Each experience, whether joyful or painful, carries lessons. When you show kindness in the face of anger, you learn compassion. When you endure heartbreak, you uncover resilience. Every choice, every consequence, every triumph and mistake—these are your teachers. And as your soul evolves, so too does its capacity for wisdom, compassion, and peace."

A warm light shimmered nearby, and the human felt a presence they couldn't see. "Is that an angel?"

"Yes," the soul said. "Angels often guide you through this process, offering whispers of wisdom and protection. They remind you of the truths your soul already knows but your human self sometimes forgets. They help you align with the higher vibrations of love, forgiveness, and purpose."

The human tilted their head, as if listening. "So what does all this say about who I am now? My soul age, or whatever you call it?"

"Soul age reflects the maturity of your wisdom," the soul replied. "An infant soul is just beginning its journey, focused on survival and discovery. A baby soul seeks order, exploring rules and traditions. A young soul is ambitious, driven by success and recognition. Mature souls, like you, turn inward, seeking meaning and authentic connection. And old souls..."

"They're the wise ones," the human interjected with a small smile.

"Yes," the soul agreed. "Old souls embody a calm, expansive understanding. They know that true wealth is not material but spiritual—found in love, connection, and the pursuit of higher truths."

The human considered this. "How do I know where I fall in all this? My soul age?"

"Start by reflecting," the soul suggested. "What drives you? Are you focused on achievement, or do you seek deeper truths? Notice the patterns in your life—the relationships, challenges, and themes that repeat. Your reactions to them reveal much about your growth."

"And angels," the human added, glancing at the light again. "Can they help me figure it out?"

"They can," the soul said. "Angels offer guidance when you're lost and clarity when the path ahead seems dark. By tuning into their presence through prayer, meditation, or quiet moments, you can receive the insights you seek. They honor your free will, but they're always there, nudging you toward alignment with your higher self."

The human smiled faintly. "It feels comforting, knowing they're around. But what should I do with all this wisdom I'm gathering?"

"Use it," the soul encouraged. "Let it shape how you live and love. Cultivate mindfulness to stay present, even in difficulty. Embrace challenges as opportunities for growth. Connect deeply with others, for relationships are sacred teachers. And above all, practice forgiveness—it lightens your spirit and allows you to move forward unburdened."

The human leaned back, gazing at the soft glow of the angelic presence. "This journey feels so much bigger than I thought. How do I trust it all?"

"By remembering," the soul whispered. "Remember that you are never alone. Your angels walk with you, offering strength and insight. Trust that every experience, no matter how difficult, serves a purpose in your evolution. And know that each choice you make, each act of love and learning, enriches not only your journey but the collective consciousness of all souls."

The human closed their eyes again, a deep sense of peace washing over them. "I think I understand now. Wisdom isn't about knowing—it's about being. About living in alignment with the lessons my soul has gathered."

"Exactly," the soul affirmed. "And as you live in this way, you become a light for others, just as angels are for you. Your wisdom becomes a gift not only to yourself but to the world. This is how we grow, together, in love and truth."

The angel's light grew brighter for a moment, as if in agreement, before softly fading into the air. The human opened their eyes, ready to embrace the path ahead, knowing it was guided by wisdom both ancient and eternal.

CHAPTER: SOUL'S JOURNEY

The twilight deepened, and the conversation between the human and their soul flowed with a rare clarity. They began to explore the layers of the soul's journey—how each step, each choice, was not just an isolated moment but part of a larger, interconnected tapestry. As they talked, the human felt an old, intuitive question rising to the surface: what was the significance of this journey across past lives, the present moment, and into the future? They felt a sense of purpose behind each step, each cycle, yet yearned to understand it more deeply.

The soul's voice resonated within the human's heart, gentle yet firm. "This journey, with its echoes of past lives and ancestral memory, the vibrance of the present, and the promise of a future, isn't just a spiritual exercise," it said, "but a profound ethical invitation to understand and fulfill who

The soul's first focus was on the concept of the past. As it spoke, the human felt a sense of ancient wisdom unfolding, as if listening to a story whispered through time. "The past holds layers of meaning," the soul said. "Consider the notion of past lives. It's found in spiritual traditions like Buddhism and Hinduism, which teach that the soul accumulates experiences, learns, and grows across multiple lives. Even in the Western world, some believe the soul travels a similar path, gathering wisdom as it moves."

The human nodded, recalling how, throughout their life, they'd occasionally felt a sense of déjà vu or unexplainable connection to people or places. "Maybe," the human mused, "these feelings are more than coincidences. Could they be echoes from a life I don't consciously remember?"

"Indeed," the soul affirmed. "Whether or not we believe in literal reincarnation, our sense of the past still shapes us. Think of your childhood, your ancestors, and even your family's cultural history. These influences carry lessons, patterns, and memories that can subtly guide you today. It's like St. Thomas Aquinas suggested: 'Our past does not determine who we are, but it does influence the choices we make.' Our past experiences—whether they're from this life or another—are threads in a greater pattern."

The human took in these words, reflecting on their life's recurring themes. "So, the past isn't just memories—it's a pattern that I'm here to recognize and, maybe, learn from?"

"Yes," replied the soul, "think of it as a mirror. By reflecting on past lives or ancestral memory, you recognize patterns that might otherwise remain hidden. These patterns can reveal insights about who you are and the deeper work your soul is here to do."

The soul shared a story of an artist who struggled with inspiration, feeling blocked and weighed down by self-doubt. One night, the artist had a dream of a place they'd never been, filled with colors and landscapes that seemed vivid and familiar. "The artist felt a pull to visit this place," the soul explained. "And when they did, they felt something awaken within them—a deep connection that inspired their work in a way they'd never experienced before. Whether it was an echo of a past life or an intuitive nudge, the past opened a new path forward."

"Reflecting on the past offers you the chance to learn from patterns," the soul continued. "Maybe you have an inexplicable talent, a recurring fear, or a bond with someone that feels ancient. Carl Jung called these elements the 'collective unconscious,' suggesting that we inherit both personal and ancestral memories. These memories, buried in our psyche, affect our beliefs and actions, often without us realizing it."

The human's mind drifted to fears they couldn't easily explain. "Could my anxieties be connected to memories from the past?"

"Exactly," said the soul. "Recognizing these echoes can reveal old wounds or lessons you've been carrying. By acknowledging them, you gain the chance to work through and heal them, so they no longer weigh you down. You can break cycles that were, until now, invisible threads."

The soul's words reminded the human of another story: that of Elijah, the prophet who encountered an angel when he was ready to give up. "Exhausted and defeated, he lay down under a tree, only to be awakened by an angel offering food and encouragement," the soul said. "That simple act gave him strength to continue. Sometimes, it's by facing the depths of our past that we find the power to keep going, even when we feel lost

As the conversation turned to the present, the human felt a shift within them, an awareness of the immediacy and power of the current moment. "So the past guides us," they said thoughtfully. "But it's here, in the present, that I have the power to change things."

The soul nodded, its presence a steady reminder of the beauty of now. "Exactly. The present moment is where you bring together all the lessons, all the wisdom, and apply them consciously. Living in the present is a deeply ethical act because it requires you to face who you are honestly and make choices that reflect your highest potential. As Aquinas believed, the ethical life is a conscious one, shaped by a commitment to grow in virtue."

They discussed mindfulness, which the soul explained as the practice of being fully in the present. "By focusing on each moment," it said, "you can quiet the noise of the past and future, allowing your inner voice to guide you. Practices like meditation or journaling help cultivate this awareness."

The human thought of times they'd felt fully alive and present—moments of peace in nature, laughter with friends, or quiet reflection. "Those are moments when I feel connected to something deeper, something beyond just myself," they admitted.

"That's your soul," the soul replied. "In these moments, you're not only grounded but growing. The present is where you integrate what you've learned from the past and use it to create a more fulfilling life. It's a space of dynamic growth, a place to choose the values and principles that align with who you truly are."

The soul shared another story, this time of a mother who, after years of emotional distance, made a conscious decision to be more present with her children. "She realized that by being fully there, listening, engaging, she was healing old wounds from her own childhood and creating a loving legacy for her family. Every mindful action became a thread that wove a stronger bond."

The conversation turned to the future, and the human felt a stirring of anticipation. "If the past is our teacher, and the present our workshop, what role does the future play in the journey?"

The soul's response was both gentle and inspiring. "The future holds the promise of all that you can become. It's the field of possibility shaped by the intentions you set and the actions you take today. By thinking of your legacy, you consider what you want to pass down—not only to those who come after you but to your future self. This is a deeply ethical practice, for it's about creating a vision that inspires and guides you."

The human remembered a quote from philosopher Jean-Paul Sartre: "Life begins on the other side of despair." They realized that by setting intentions and creating a vision for the future, they were choosing hope, resilience, and purpose over fear.

The soul smiled within them, sensing the depth of their understanding. "Yes. Consider each choice you make today as a seed that will grow into your legacy. By choosing to live with integrity and intention, you create a legacy that reflects your highest values. And remember, legacy isn't just about grand gestures; it's found in daily kindnesses, in moments of honesty and compassion."

They spoke of examples—the environmentalist planting trees, the teacher nurturing students, the healer caring for others. Each was creating a future filled with hope and meaning, a legacy of purpose that would touch others even after they were gone.

As the stars appeared, the human felt the full weight and wonder of the soul's journey. The past, present, and future were no longer isolated moments but interconnected threads weaving a sacred tapestry of existence.

The soul spoke one last time, its voice filled with both wisdom and love. "By healing the past, living mindfully in the present, and setting intentions for the future, you are engaging in a journey that transcends you. Your choices are threads that shape not only your life but the lives of countless others."

In that quiet moment, the human felt an overwhelming sense of peace, realizing that every choice, every moment, was a sacred step in the unfolding story of their soul's journey. With a deep breath, they embraced the timeless journey, knowing that they were part of something far greater than themselves, something that stretched across time and space, filled with purpose and meaning.

CHAPTER: ETERNAL RHYTHMS: THE SOUL'S CYCLICAL PATH

The human sat quietly, staring out at the horizon where the sky met the ocean. "Why does it all feel so cyclical?" they asked, their voice tinged with curiosity. "Life, death, the moments in between—it's as if I'm moving through a loop, but each time, I'm a little different."

The soul's voice answered, calm and knowing. "You are. What you're sensing are the soul cycles—the stages your soul moves through across lifetimes. Each cycle is a chapter in the endless journey of your growth, a rhythm of experience, reflection, and evolution."

The human turned their gaze downward, drawing patterns in the sand. "Tell me about these cycles. What are they really?"

"They're like the seasons," the soul explained, "each with its own purpose and lessons. They begin with incarnation—the moment your soul chooses to embody a physical form. Each life you enter isn't random; it's chosen with intention. Your soul picks the circumstances, relationships, and challenges to learn something new or balance karma from previous lives."

The human raised an eyebrow. "Wait, you're saying I chose this life? All of it?"

"Yes," the soul said gently. "You chose it to grow. Life on Earth is a school, and each incarnation is a new course. Sometimes it's joy and love; other times, it's hardship and loss. But every experience carries a lesson, and through these lessons, your soul evolves."

"So what happens after incarnation?" the human asked, leaning forward as if to catch every word.

"After incarnation comes growth and learning," the soul continued. "This is where you navigate life—the challenges, the triumphs, the relationships. Each moment teaches you about resilience, compassion, trust, and the many facets of love. You're like a sculptor, chipping away at the rough edges to reveal your true essence."

The human thought for a moment. "And what about those moments where everything seems... different? Like I'm waking up to something bigger?"

"That's the awakening phase," the soul said with a smile in its voice. "At some point in each cycle, there's an awakening—a shift where you begin to remember who you truly are beyond the physical world. It might be triggered by a profound event, a spiritual practice, or simply an inner longing for more. In awakening, you start to see beyond the surface of life and connect with your spiritual nature."

The human nodded slowly. "I think I've felt that before. It's like a quiet pull, a reminder that there's more."

"Exactly," the soul affirmed. "And with that awareness often comes a desire for service and contribution. This is when you feel called to share your gifts, help others, and make a positive impact. It could be through your work, your relationships, or simply the kindness you offer to those around you. In giving, your soul expands."

"And then?" the human asked softly.

"Then comes reflection and integration," the soul said. "Near the end of an incarnation, your soul looks back on the journey—taking stock of the lessons, the growth, and the love shared. It's a time for release, forgiveness, and gratitude. The experiences of the life are woven into the fabric of your soul, enriching it for the cycles yet to come."

The human leaned back, letting the waves lap at their feet. "And when it's over? When the body dies?"

"That's the transition," the soul replied, its tone tender. "Death isn't an ending; it's a return to the spiritual realm. There, your soul reviews the life you lived—not in judgment, but in understanding. You see the ripples of your choices, the impact you've had, and the wisdom you've gained. And then, when the time is right, the next cycle begins."

The human let out a breath, their eyes distant. "It's a lot to take in. But it's... beautiful. Like everything has a purpose, even the hard parts."

"It does," the soul assured them. "Every phase—every joy, every challenge—is a part of your growth. And your legacy isn't just what you leave behind in the physical world. It's the wisdom you carry forward, the love you've shared, and the creative expressions of your soul. Your art, your acts of kindness, even your struggles—they all add to the tapestry of your eternal journey."

The human smiled faintly. "So even when life feels messy, it's still part of something bigger?"

"Always," the soul said. "The cycles are a reminder that you're never stuck. You're always moving, evolving, and contributing to the greater whole. And as you grow, so does the collective consciousness. Your journey uplifts others, just as theirs uplifts you."

The human looked out at the sea again, a sense of calm washing over them. "How do I make the most of it? Of these cycles?"

"Be present," the soul advised. "Live fully in each moment, even the difficult ones, because they carry the seeds of transformation. Treat yourself with compassion—growth takes time, and mistakes are part of the process. Connect deeply with others; they're your fellow travelers, each teaching and learning alongside you. And above all, trust your soul's path. It knows the way."

The human closed their eyes, breathing in the salty air. "It feels like I'm starting to understand. This journey... it's not about getting somewhere, is it?"

"No," the soul said softly. "It's about being. Each cycle is an unfolding, a becoming. And through it all, your essence—your light—grows brighter, drawing you closer to the truth of who you are. You are infinite, and so is your journey."

The human sat in silence, the rhythm of the waves echoing the rhythm of their own soul, both timeless and eternal.

STORY: THE ECHOES OF ETERNITY

In the quiet coastal town of Seabrook, where the waves whispered secrets to the shore and the moonlight danced on the water, there existed an old lighthouse known as the Beacon of Souls. Legends said it was a place where the boundaries between past lives and present existence blurred, and where one could catch glimpses of their soul's journey through its many cycles and phases.

Enter Clara Hawthorne, a writer with a penchant for the mystical. Clara had always felt an inexplicable pull toward Seabrook, as if her soul had roots in its ancient sands. After inheriting a small cottage from her grandmother, she decided to make Seabrook her home, hoping to find inspiration for her next novel.

One stormy evening, Clara was drawn to the Beacon of Souls. Its light cut through the darkness, a solitary sentinel against the tempest. She wrapped herself in a thick coat and made her way up the winding path, the wind howling around her.

As she approached the lighthouse, Clara noticed an old, leather-bound journal half-buried in the sand. Intrigued, she picked it up and dusted it off. The journal's cover was inscribed with the words, "Echoes of Eternity." She opened it to find delicate, handwritten entries detailing the lives of various individuals—each entry a snapshot of a different soul phase.

Inside, the journal was filled with stories of birth, life, death, and rebirth—each cycle revealing the soul's evolution and lessons learned. One entry in particular caught her eye, a name that sent a shiver down her spine: "Clara Hawthorne."

"How is this possible?" Clara whispered to herself, her heart racing. She read on, finding detailed accounts of her own life, from her childhood memories to her deepest fears and dreams. But it didn't stop there—the journal also recounted lives she had no conscious memory of, lifetimes spent in distant lands, facing joys and trials that shaped her soul.

The journal spoke of soul cycles—the phases each soul goes through in its eternal journey. Infant souls, grappling with survival and fear. Young souls, driven by ambition and success. Mature souls, seeking deeper connections and understanding. And old souls, wise and serene, having seen the world through many eyes.

As Clara delved deeper into the journal, she discovered a recurring theme: a mysterious figure known only as The Watcher, a guardian of souls who guided them through their cycles. Intrigued and a bit unsettled, she decided to investigate further.

The next day, Clara visited the local library to see if she could find any mention of The Watcher. The librarian, an elderly woman named Edith, seemed to know more than she let on.

"Ah, the Beacon of Souls and The Watcher," Edith said with a knowing smile. "Many have sought to unravel its mysteries. The Watcher is said to be a timeless guardian, ensuring that souls learn their lessons and move through their cycles."

Clara's curiosity was piqued. "Do you know where I can find more about this Watcher?"

Edith leaned in, her voice a hushed whisper. "Legend has it that The Watcher can be contacted through a ritual at the lighthouse during the full moon. Tonight is such a night."

That evening, as the full moon cast its silver light over Seabrook, Clara returned to the lighthouse. She carried the journal with her, feeling a strange sense of anticipation. Inside the lighthouse, she found an ancient, circular mosaic on the floor, depicting the phases of the soul.

Following the instructions she had found in the journal, Clara lit a circle of candles around the mosaic and stood in the center. She closed her eyes and focused on the intention of connecting with The Watcher.

SOUL PROTECTORS

A soft, warm light filled the room, and a figure emerged from the shadows—a tall, cloaked figure with eyes that seemed to hold the wisdom of the ages.

"Clara," The Watcher spoke, their voice a harmonious blend of many tones. "You have questions about your soul's journey."

Clara nodded, her heart pounding. "Yes, I want to understand my soul cycles and the phases I've been through."

The Watcher raised a hand, and the room filled with visions of Clara's past lives. She saw herself as a warrior, a healer, a scholar, and a mother. Each life carried its own lessons, its own triumphs and sorrows. She felt the weight of each cycle, the growth and wisdom they had imparted to her soul.

"The phases of your soul are like the seasons," The Watcher explained. "Each one is necessary for your growth and evolution. You are currently in the mature phase, seeking deeper understanding and connection. But know this: the journey is eternal, and each phase brings you closer to the essence of your true self."

Clara felt tears well up in her eyes, a mix of awe and relief. "What should I do now?" she asked.

"Embrace your journey," The Watcher said. "Continue to learn, to grow, and to connect with others. Your legacy is not just in your actions, but in the wisdom you share and the love you spread."

With that, the light began to fade, and The Watcher disappeared, leaving Clara alone in the lighthouse. She felt a profound sense of peace and purpose, knowing that her soul's journey was guided by forces beyond her understanding.

In the days that followed, Clara wrote her novel, weaving in the themes of soul cycles and the lessons she had learned. Her story resonated with readers far and wide, touching souls and inspiring others to explore their own journeys.

And as the Beacon of Souls continued to shine its light over Seabrook, Clara knew that she was never truly alone. Her soul was part of an eternal cycle, guided by the whispers of the past and the promise of the future.

CHAPTER: MENDING THE FRAGMENTED SOUL

The human sat in a dimly lit room, their head bowed as if the weight of the world pressed down on their shoulders. "I feel... hollow," they murmured. "Like something inside me is missing. I don't know how to explain it, but I'm not whole."

The soul's voice came gently, wrapping around the human like a comforting embrace. "You're feeling the effects of soul loss. A part of you, your essence, has stepped away, seeking safety from the pain you've endured."

"Soul loss?" The human lifted their gaze, confusion and curiosity flickering in their eyes. "What does that mean? How can I lose part of my soul?"

"It happens when the pain is too great, the trauma too sharp," the soul explained. "In moments of intense grief, fear, or despair, pieces of your soul may fragment to protect you. It's a survival mechanism, a way to shield your core from being overwhelmed."

The human nodded slowly, a memory of deep loss surfacing. "Like when I lost them," they whispered, their voice breaking.

"Yes," the soul replied. "The death of a loved one, heartbreak, even prolonged stress—all these can lead to soul loss. And while it keeps you safe in the moment, over time, the disconnection leaves you feeling empty, like something vital is missing."

A soft light appeared in the corner of the room, and the human turned toward it. "Is that an angel?"

"It is," the soul confirmed. "Angels often come to those experiencing soul loss. They bring comfort, guidance, and a reminder that even in your pain, you are never truly alone. Do you feel their presence?"

The human closed their eyes and breathed deeply. "Yes," they said after a moment. "It feels... warm. Like they're holding me without touching me."

The soul's voice softened further. "That's their love, their light. They are here to help you remember your strength and to guide you back to yourself."

"But how do I know for sure it's soul loss?" the human asked. "I mean, couldn't this just be... life? Stress? Depression?"

"It can be hard to tell," the soul admitted, "but there are signs. Do you feel disconnected from the world around you? From your own emotions?"

"Yes," the human said, their voice barely a whisper.

"Do you feel empty, like something essential is missing?"

A tear slipped down their cheek. "Yes."

"And what about fatigue?" the soul continued. "Do you feel drained, even when you've rested? Or like you're carrying a weight you can't explain?"

"All the time," the human confessed.

The angel's light grew brighter, a quiet affirmation of the soul's words.

"It's not your fault," the soul assured. "You've experienced deep wounds—losses, stresses, traumas—that have taken pieces of you. But just as they've left, they can return. Healing is possible."

The human glanced toward the angel's light, a flicker of hope igniting in their eyes. "How? How do I heal from this?"

"First, seek guidance," the soul said. "There are healers—shamans, spiritual practitioners, even certain therapists—who understand soul loss and can help you reclaim the missing parts of yourself. This process is called soul retrieval."

The human nodded. "And what can I do for myself?"

"Begin with self-care," the soul advised. "Spend time in nature, where the Earth's energy can ground and heal you. Create a sacred space for reflection, meditation, and prayer. Allow yourself to feel, fully and deeply, without judgment. Suppressed emotions only build walls between you and your lost fragments."

The angel's light pulsed softly, and the human felt a wave of peace wash over them. "And the angel? How do they help?"

"Angels guide you toward the light within yourself," the soul explained. "They offer strength when you feel weak, clarity when you feel lost. In moments of despair, call upon them. They are always near, waiting to assist."

The human closed their eyes again, this time with purpose. "I want to try. To call on them."

"Do so," the soul encouraged. "Feel their presence, their unwavering love. And as you do, imagine the lost pieces of your soul returning, like stars finding their way back to the sky."

A soft, melodic whisper filled the room, the angel's voice answering the unspoken call. The human felt warmth bloom in their chest, a sensation of something long absent stirring within.

"I think..." they began, tears streaming freely now. "I think I can feel it. A part of me coming back."

The soul's voice was steady and kind. "This is just the beginning. Be patient with yourself. Healing is a journey, not a destination. Trust the process and the angels who walk beside you."

The human opened their eyes, the glow of the angel's light reflecting in them. "I don't feel so alone anymore. Maybe... maybe I can do this."

"You can," the soul affirmed. "Because even in the deepest moments of soul loss, the light within you never truly fades. With time, love, and the guidance of angels, you will find your way back to wholeness."

The angel's light lingered a moment longer, then began to fade, leaving the human bathed in a quiet sense of peace and possibility. They placed a hand over their heart, ready to take the first step toward reclaiming their soul.

STORY: THE WHISPERS OF MIDNIGHT

In the quiet town of Willowbrook, nestled among ancient oaks and mist-laden hills, strange occurrences were unfolding. Willowbrook was a place where time seemed to stand still, and secrets lingered like the morning fog. But lately, something even more mysterious had begun to seep into its tranquil streets—people were losing pieces of their souls.

Elena Martin, a young woman with a talent for the extraordinary, had always felt an otherworldly connection to the unseen. As a child, she often spoke of angels who visited her dreams, bringing messages of comfort and guidance. Now, as an adult, she was known in town as a healer, someone who could sense the unspoken and mend the broken.

One crisp autumn evening, as the first whispers of midnight approached, Elena received a call from an old friend, Sheriff Tom Hawkins. He sounded perplexed, his voice a mix of concern and bewilderment.

"Elena, something strange is happening," Tom said. "People are experiencing... I don't know how to describe it. It's like they're missing parts of themselves. They speak of feeling empty, disconnected. I need your help."

Elena's heart quickened. She had heard stories of soul loss before but never encountered it so close to home. She agreed to meet Tom at the old Johnson farmhouse, where the latest victim, Mrs. Agnes Parker, had been found in a state of deep despair.

Arriving at the farmhouse, Elena was struck by the eerie stillness that hung in the air. Mrs. Parker, usually a vibrant woman despite her age, sat slumped in a chair, her eyes vacant and lifeless.

"Mrs. Parker, it's Elena," she whispered softly, taking the old woman's hand. "Can you tell me what happened?"

Agnes's gaze slowly shifted to Elena, a flicker of recognition in her eyes. "It was the shadow," she murmured. "A shadow that took a part of me. I could feel it pulling away my very essence."

Elena nodded, feeling a chill run down her spine. "Don't worry, Mrs. Parker. We'll get it back."

As the night deepened, Elena retreated to her small, candlelit room at the edge of the woods. She knew she needed to call upon the angels for guidance. Closing her eyes, she began to meditate, focusing her thoughts on Archangel Raphael, the healer.

"Raphael, please help me find the lost souls of Willowbrook. Guide me to restore what has been taken."

A warm, gentle light filled the room, and a voice, clear and soothing, resonated in her mind. "Elena, the shadow you seek is not of this world. It is a remnant of an ancient curse, one that preys on the vulnerabilities of the human soul. You must seek the Well of Echoes, where the veil between realms is thin."

The Well of Echoes was a place of legend, hidden deep within the Whispering Woods. It was said to be a conduit between the physical world and the spiritual realm, a place where the boundaries of reality blurred.

With renewed determination, Elena set out at dawn, guided by an unearthly intuition. The Whispering Woods were dense and foreboding, but she felt a protective presence, like unseen hands guiding her steps.

As she approached the well, Elena noticed a figure standing in the clearing—a tall, ethereal being bathed in light. It was Archangel Raphael, his wings shimmering with divine energy.

"Elena, you have done well to come here," Raphael said. "The shadow you seek dwells within the depths of the well. It feeds on the lost and the forgotten. You must descend and confront it, but fear not, for I will be with you."

Taking a deep breath, Elena climbed down into the well, her heart pounding with a mixture of fear and resolve. The air grew colder, and the light above faded, leaving her in near darkness. Yet she felt Raphael's presence, a beacon of hope in the gloom.

At the bottom of the well, a swirling darkness awaited her. The shadow, amorphous and malevolent, writhed as if aware of her presence. Elena focused her thoughts, calling upon Raphael's strength.

"By the power of light and love, I command you to release the souls you have taken!"

The shadow hissed, its form contorting, but the presence of Raphael's light was overwhelming. The darkness began to recede, revealing faint, luminous shapes—fragments of the souls it had consumed.

One by one, the soul fragments floated upwards, drawn back to their rightful owners. The shadow, weakened and diminished, dissipated into nothingness.

Emerging from the well, Elena felt a profound sense of relief. The angels had guided her, and the lost souls of Willowbrook were beginning to heal. She returned to the farmhouse, where Mrs. Parker and others affected by the soul loss were already showing signs of recovery.

As the sun rose over Willowbrook, casting its warm glow over the town, Elena knew that the angels had once again helped her to restore balance and light. She felt grateful for their presence and the mystery that had brought her closer to understanding the profound connections between the human soul and the divine.

In the days that followed, Willowbrook began to heal, its residents finding new strength and purpose. And Elena, with her bond to the angels even stronger, continued her work as a healer, knowing that whenever darkness threatened, the light would always prevail.

CHAPTER: ANGELS AMONG US: SIGNS, WONDERS AND VISITATIONS

As the human wandered through a quiet place of reflection, an inner presence—one they knew as their soul—stirred with a question, drawing them inward. "Tell me," the soul began, "have you ever wondered about those moments in life that feel... like a gentle touch from beyond? A guiding force, a flash of clarity that seems otherworldly?" The human paused, thinking of times when they felt supported in ways they couldn't explain, as though a light beyond comprehension had reached them.

With a sense of reverence, they responded, "Are you speaking of angels? I've heard stories, but I don't know if I've ever encountered one myself. Those accounts often feel elusive, like they belong to someone else's world."

"Yet angels aren't as far from you as you might think," the soul replied, its voice filled with wisdom and a hint of playfulness. "These encounters don't always come with wings and halos; they can arrive in a glance, a whisper, a stranger's kindness, or even in a dream. They're signs and symbols, messages from the divine—catalysts for the soul's evolution."

The soul's words brought to mind a story the human had once read, one where an angel appeared to a wanderer on a desolate path, illuminating their way and filling them with strength just as they'd begun to lose hope. "Sometimes," the soul said, sensing the human's recollection, "these encounters are grand, leaving no doubt in your mind that you've touched something divine. Other times, they're so subtle that you may only notice their significance in hindsight."

The human, intrigued, wanted to understand more about how these encounters played out across different beliefs and spiritual practices. "Different traditions see angels in various ways, right? But isn't the essence of these encounters similar?"

"Yes," the soul agreed. "Take the mystics and saints of Christianity, for instance. Angels are often viewed as messengers, guiding figures who appear in moments of great decision or turmoil. St. Thomas Aquinas saw angels as pure intellect, beings who, though invisible, could reach human beings in ways that transform and guide their spiritual journeys. For him, angelic encounters were profound gifts of knowledge, an alignment with divine wisdom meant to steer us on the path of truth."

"And in other traditions?" the human asked, intrigued by the soul's insights.

"In Islam, angels are considered close to God, each with specific roles and duties," the soul explained. "Encounters with angels, like the angel Gabriel who visited the Prophet Muhammad, represent moments when the divine breaks through the human world, offering guidance and revelation. The purpose of these encounters is transformation—a reminder of the soul's journey and connection to the divine."

The human felt a deep resonance, imagining how, in each of these traditions, such moments were transformative. "So, these encounters seem to be invitations—a way to see beyond ourselves?"

"Precisely," the soul continued. "And it's not just in monotheistic religions. In Buddhism, for instance, the concept of bodhisattvas—enlightened beings who choose to help others reach enlightenment—mirrors this idea. While not always described as angels, these guides perform a similar function, appearing as catalysts for those ready to awaken further on their path."

The human began to understand that angelic encounters, however one chose to interpret them, served as reminders of something greater, a purpose beyond the everyday. "These stories make me think of those moments in my own life when things seemed to shift. I didn't see an angel, but I felt guided, like something was watching over me."

The soul was pleased to hear this acknowledgment. "There are countless ways in which these presences make themselves known. Not all encounters are dramatic. Sometimes, they're like a gentle nudge when you least expect it, a sense of peace or clarity during a challenging time. They are what I call 'angelic whispers.' They come in dreams, sudden realizations, or quiet moments of reflection."

The human remembered a time when they'd felt an overwhelming sense of peace, an inner certainty that things would be okay, despite feeling lost. "There was this one night when I felt... something. I was at my lowest, but somehow, this calm washed over me. It felt like I wasn't alone, as if someone or something was watching over me."

"That," the soul said warmly, "was an angelic encounter. It may not have been a grand appearance, but it was a presence, nonetheless—a moment designed to bring you back to yourself, to remind you of your strength and the light within you. Angelic encounters are not always about physical form; they're about essence, a quiet reassurance that the journey is sacred and that you're not alone."

The human felt a wave of gratitude, realizing that they may have been touched by these forces more than they'd recognized. "It's comforting to think of it that way, that these presences are there when we need them, guiding us in ways we might only understand in hindsight."

The soul gently probed further. "Yes, and it's in these encounters—be they dramatic or subtle—that the soul finds new ways to evolve. These moments offer more than reassurance; they prompt reflection, nudging you toward growth. As the Jewish mystics describe, each encounter with an angel is like touching a divine spark, a reminder that there is something sacred to seek within yourself."

Reflecting on this, the human began to understand that these encounters were invitations to deeper understanding and growth. "So these presences, these angels, are part of the journey—a way of helping us reach a deeper purpose?"

"Exactly," replied the soul, with a sense of satisfaction. "Think of them as signposts along the way, reminders that your life is connected to something larger. They encourage you to look inward, to find the divine within. They may not change your path for you, but they'll offer clarity, reassurance, or wisdom that helps you evolve, bringing you closer to your true essence."

The human felt as if they were glimpsing a hidden layer of existence, one where angels, guides, and divine presences were all subtly orchestrating their path. "Maybe I've been so focused on looking for concrete answers that I've missed the guidance already around me. I've been waiting for a dramatic encounter, but perhaps I should start listening for those whispers."

The soul's presence seemed to glow with approval. "Yes, for each moment of stillness is an opportunity to hear those angelic whispers, those gentle nudges reminding you of the soul's evolution. Like a candle in the dark, each encounter sheds light on a new facet of yourself, a way to grow, to understand, to become."

With that, the human felt a sense of deep peace. They understood now that angelic encounters weren't confined to grand visions or mystical revelations but lived within moments of grace, a quiet sense of guidance that could emerge in anyone's life. It wasn't about seeing angels with wings but recognizing the presence of something divine in those seemingly small moments—a quiet catalyst helping them to grow, evolve, and reach toward their highest self.

CHAPTER: TIMELESS ENCOUNTERS: RELATIONSHIPS SPANNING LIFETIMES

As the human sat in quiet contemplation, they felt a subtle stirring within, a familiar presence awakening. It was as though an ancient whisper rose up from the depths of their soul, inviting them into an intimate conversation. They could feel it—a gentle, steady current urging them to explore thoughts they had rarely given voice. They closed their eyes, leaning into the sensation, and allowed the soul's presence to flow over them.

"You've felt it, haven't you?" the soul murmured, a warmth wrapping around their mind like a comforting embrace. "That sense of connection that goes beyond mere chance. Some people come into your life, and you feel as though you've met before, as if they carry some hidden meaning or purpose."

The human reflected, recalling those moments when an unexpected bond tugged at them, resonating deep within. Memories of faces, voices, and encounters filled their mind, some bringing joy, others pain, yet all carrying that distinct feeling of depth. "Yes," they replied softly. "There are people who seem to touch something inside me that no one else can reach. But... I don't always understand why they're here."

"Not all things are meant to be understood at first glance," the soul said, its tone carrying both wisdom and patience. "The truth is, each connection has a purpose, even if it's not immediately clear. These souls are placed on your path not randomly, but with intention. They help you discover different facets of yourself—your strengths, your vulnerabilities, even parts of yourself you've hidden away."

The human nodded, thinking back to times when certain connections had changed them deeply. Friendships that felt like a mirror, relationships that challenged them, and even brief encounters that lingered for reasons they couldn't explain. "It's like each person who enters my life is a part of a larger picture," they whispered, trying to grasp the idea. "But sometimes, I don't know if they're meant to stay or if they're just passing through."

"Let me tell you about the different kinds of connections," the soul continued, as though guiding them on a journey through the depths of their own heart. "Each one has a role in your evolution. Some are there to bring you peace and understanding, while others are meant to challenge you, forcing you to confront parts of yourself you'd rather ignore. And there are those who simply resonate with you, bringing ease and familiarity without the need for anything more."

The soul began, gently, with the concept of soulmates. "Soulmates are often misunderstood," it explained. "Many people believe they are romantic partners alone, but soulmates can be so much more. They are anyone with whom you share a profound connection, those who come into your life to help you grow, experience love, and expand your understanding of yourself. Soulmates may be lovers, yes, but they can also be friends, family, or mentors."

The human thought about the friends who felt like kindred spirits—those who seemed to understand them without needing words, people with whom they could share their truest thoughts and deepest dreams. "So, it's not just romance," they mused aloud. "A soulmate can be anyone who feels... like a part of me, someone who just understands."

"Yes," the soul affirmed, "a soulmate connection is marked by a feeling of recognition, a sense of ease. With a soulmate friend, there's an unspoken understanding. And with family members, sometimes there's a bond that goes beyond the ordinary ties of blood. You may feel as though you've known them across lifetimes, bound by an invisible thread that connects you through time."

The human smiled, feeling a warmth settle over their heart as they thought of family members who felt like anchors, people who knew them at a soul level and offered unwavering support. "I can think of a few," they whispered. "People who have always been there, who feel like a safe harbor."

The soul paused, as if savoring this feeling, then gently shifted the conversation to a different type of connection—one that carried both intensity and challenge. "Now, let me tell you about twin flames," it said, its tone deepening. "This connection is unlike the gentleness of a soulmate. Twin flames are not here to simply offer comfort or ease; they are here to ignite transformation. They're often described as two halves of the same soul, split across different bodies, destined to find each other in order to grow and evolve."

The human's heart quickened, recalling a relationship that had been both passionate and tumultuous. The intensity was undeniable, as if a fire had sparked that neither of them could control. "That sounds... familiar," they admitted, a touch of sadness in their voice. "It was powerful, but it wasn't easy. It felt like they were a mirror, showing me all the parts of myself I didn't want to see."

"That's exactly it," the soul agreed. "A twin flame will reflect both your light and your shadows. They come into your life to help you confront your deepest fears, unresolved wounds, and hidden potential. They challenge you, provoke you, sometimes even push you to the edge. This is a connection built on the foundation of growth, and growth, as you know, is rarely comfortable."

The human sighed, understanding the depth of this truth. That relationship had pushed them to their limits, forcing them to confront emotions they had buried for years. "It felt like a storm," they murmured. "As if they were there to shake me awake."

"Yes," the soul responded gently. "And though it may be painful, this connection holds the potential for profound transformation. Twin flames are meant to help you reach your highest self, to burn away the illusions and reveal the truth of who you are."

The human allowed this to settle, realizing that perhaps the turbulence they had experienced was not a sign of failure but part of a larger process of growth. They were beginning to see the wisdom in each connection, even those that had brought pain.

After a pause, the soul continued, its voice softer now, speaking of karmic relationships. "These are relationships bound by karma, often stretching across lifetimes. They are built on the principle of unfinished business. If you've ever felt trapped in a loop, finding yourself drawn to similar people or repeating patterns in your relationships, it might be due to a karmic bond."

The human frowned, recalling relationships that seemed to follow a similar script, bringing the same challenges and heartache. "I've noticed that," they admitted. "Sometimes, it feels like I keep ending up in the same place, no matter how much I try to change."

"That's the essence of a karmic relationship," the soul explained. "These connections are here to help you resolve lessons you left unfinished. They may be intense, even painful, but they carry valuable insights. Each time you encounter a karmic partner, you're given another chance to break free from the cycle. These relationships are rarely meant to last forever, but the growth they bring is enduring."

The human felt a sense of relief, as though a weight had been lifted. It wasn't that they were doomed to repeat the same mistakes—it was that each repetition was an opportunity to learn, to finally heal and move forward. "So, there's a purpose to the patterns," they said, feeling a new sense of hope.

"Yes," the soul replied, its voice filled with compassion. "Every pattern holds a lesson, and once you learn it, you can let go and step into a new chapter."

After a moment, the soul's tone lightened, moving on to kindred spirits—those connections that brought ease and joy. "Not every connection is so intense," it said with a gentle laugh, sensing the human's need for respite. "There are also kindred spirits, those who resonate with you on a level that feels simple and joyful. These are the people who share your values, your interests, and your outlook on life. With a kindred spirit, there's an immediate sense of ease. Conversations flow naturally, and being in their presence feels like a breath of fresh air."

The human felt a smile tug at their lips, recalling friends who brought laughter and lightness into their life. "Yes," they agreed. "With them, it's just... easy."

"Exactly," the soul affirmed. "Kindred spirits are like companions on your journey, offering support and understanding without demands. They're reminders that not all connections are here to challenge you—some are simply here to share joy, to remind you of the beauty of companionship."

Feeling lighter, the human listened as the soul went on to describe soul teachers—those individuals who entered their life at crucial moments, often bringing guidance or wisdom. "These are the people who appear when you need them most," the soul explained. "They may not stay forever, but their words or actions leave a lasting impact. Sometimes they're mentors, other times they're strangers with just the right advice. They come to teach you, to open your eyes to new perspectives."

The human thought back to a teacher whose words had changed their life's course, nudging them toward a path that felt true. "They didn't stay, but their influence is still with me," they mused, understanding that even brief encounters could shape their journey in profound ways.

The soul's presence deepened as it spoke of soul companions—those steadfast figures who provided support, stability, and love. "These are the ones who journey through life with you," it said warmly. "They are like a safe harbor, offering consistency and understanding. With a soul companion, you find a bond that endures through the ups and downs, someone who truly knows your heart and stays beside you."

The human felt a swell of gratitude, thinking of those who had been by their side through every trial, offering unwavering support. "They are a gift," they whispered, realizing the beauty of those who'd traveled with them.

CHAPTER: SANCTUARIES OF THE SOUL: SPACES THAT HEAL AND INSPIRE

The human wandered through the forest, each step cushioned by the soft moss beneath their feet. "Why do I feel so at ease here?" they murmured.

A quiet voice emerged within, gentle and serene. "Because this place calls to your soul. It's not just the forest—it's a sacred connection. You've found a glimpse of your soul place."

The human paused, their gaze sweeping over the sun-dappled trees. "A soul place? What does that mean?"

"It's where your soul feels most at home," the voice replied. "A space where everything aligns—peace, connection, authenticity. It's not always a physical location, though sometimes it is. It's a sanctuary for your spirit."

The human sat on a fallen log, letting the words sink in. "But what makes a place sacred to the soul? Is it the beauty? The quiet?"

"Not just that," the voice explained. "A soul place resonates with something deep within you. It's where the masks fall away, where you feel alive and whole. For some, it's a forest like this one. For others, it might be a temple, a quiet corner at home, or even a dreamscape accessed through meditation. The magic lies in the connection, not the form."

The human's brow furrowed. "But how do I know it's my soul place? How does it feel?"

"You'll know," the soul assured them. "It feels like stepping into an ancient memory you didn't realize you carried. The noise of the world fades, and there's only peace. It's a space where you can just be—authentic and free. Your thoughts slow, your heart opens, and you feel a deep connection to everything around you."

The human closed their eyes, listening to the rustling leaves and distant bird calls. "I think I feel it now. But... is it always this quiet and serene?"

"Not always," the soul said. "A soul place isn't defined by stillness or beauty alone. It's about how it speaks to you. A bustling city street can be someone's soul place if it stirs their creativity and passion. What matters is that it nurtures your spirit and aligns with your essence."

The human opened their eyes and tilted their head. "So, is it always physical? Or can it be... imaginary?"

"It can be both," the soul explained. "For some, their soul place exists in their mind—a vivid inner landscape crafted through dreams or meditation. Others feel it in sacred spaces, like temples or ancient ruins where timeless energy lingers. Some find it in nature, where the earth's rhythms align with their own. And for a few, it's a personal sanctuary they've created—a room, a corner, or even a single chair where their spirit can rest."

The human smiled faintly. "I think I've had places like that—a little reading nook, or the shore by my childhood home. They always felt... special, like they held pieces of me."

"Exactly," the soul said warmly. "Those places hold a part of your essence. They offer connection, healing, and sometimes, transformation. Your soul place is where you can process old wounds, find clarity, and grow."

The human's expression grew thoughtful. "But how do I find a soul place if I don't already know where it is?"

"It's an intuitive journey," the soul replied. "Start by listening to your heart. What places call to you, even if you don't understand why? Trust that pull. Spend time in nature and notice where you feel the most peace. If you can't travel, create a sacred space at home—a corner where you meditate, reflect, or simply be. And don't forget to journey inward. Meditation and visualization can reveal landscapes of the soul, places rich with meaning and comfort."

The human nodded. "So it's about feeling, not thinking?"

"Yes," the soul affirmed. "Your soul place is where logic steps aside and your heart takes the lead. It's about trust—trusting what feels right, what resonates deeply, even if you can't explain it."

The human stood, brushing their hands on their jeans. "And once I find it? What then?"

"Once you find your soul place," the voice said, "let it become your sanctuary. Visit it when you need clarity, peace, or renewal. Let it be a reminder of who you truly are—a place to shed the weight of the world and reconnect with your essence. And if it's a physical place, cherish and honor it. If it's within you, return to it often in your heart and mind. It's a gift, this connection to the sacred."

The human gazed at the forest around them, a smile spreading across their face. "I think I understand. It's not just a place—it's a feeling, a state of being."

"Yes," the soul agreed. "Your soul place isn't just where you go—it's where you are. It's where your spirit feels alive, where the universe feels close, and where you remember what it means to simply be. When you find it, you've found a piece of home."

The human lingered for a moment longer, breathing in the forest air, before turning to leave. But as they walked away, they carried the quiet resonance of the soul place with them, knowing they could always return—whether in body or in spirit.

STORY:THE ENIGMA OF THE SACRED GROVE

In the quaint town of Everwood, where the air smelled of pine and the rivers sang ancient songs, there was a long-held legend about a sacred place known as the Soul Grove. It was whispered among the townsfolk that the Grove was where souls found their true essence, a mystical sanctuary hidden deep within the forest, accessible only to those who were truly seeking.

Ellie Matthews, a curious and adventurous young artist, had recently moved to Everwood, drawn by the town's enchanting beauty and its promise of inspiration. She had heard murmurs about the Soul Grove, a place where one could connect with their deepest self, but most dismissed it as mere folklore.

One evening, as the sun dipped below the horizon and the sky turned to twilight, Ellie found an old, tattered map in a second-hand bookstore. It was tucked between the pages of a dusty book titled "Echoes of the Ancient Wood." The map, marked with cryptic symbols and a path leading to a heart-shaped grove, intrigued her. At the bottom, in delicate script, were the words: "Find your sacred soul place."

Ellie's heart raced with excitement. Could this be the legendary Soul Grove? She decided then and there to follow the map, eager to uncover the secrets it held.

The next morning, armed with her sketchbook and a sense of adventure, Ellie set off into the forest. The path was winding and overgrown, but she felt a strange pull, as if an invisible thread was guiding her steps. The deeper she ventured, the quieter the world became, the only sounds being the rustle of leaves and the distant call of a raven.

Hours passed, and Ellie found herself in a part of the forest she had never seen before. The air felt different here, charged with an ancient energy. She reached a clearing where the trees formed a perfect circle around a small, crystal-clear pond. The sight took her breath away. This had to be the Soul Grove.

As she stepped into the clearing, Ellie felt a wave of calm wash over her. She sat by the pond, closed her eyes, and let the serenity of the place envelop her. Time seemed to stand still, and she felt herself drifting into a meditative state.

Suddenly, she heard a gentle voice, barely more than a whisper, carried on the breeze. "Welcome, seeker."

Ellie opened her eyes to see a figure standing at the edge of the grove, bathed in soft, ethereal light. It was an elderly woman, her hair silver and her eyes shimmering with wisdom. She introduced herself as Mira, the guardian of the Soul Grove.

"You've found your way here, Ellie," Mira said, her voice as soothing as a lullaby. "This is your sacred soul place, where you can connect with the deepest parts of your being."

Ellie felt an overwhelming sense of familiarity, as if she had been here before. "But how? Why did I feel drawn here?" she asked.

Mira smiled gently. "Each soul has a place where it feels truly at home, a sanctuary where it can reflect and grow. The Soul Grove calls to those who are ready to embrace their true essence. You have been seeking, and now you are ready."

Ellie spent the next few days in the Grove, guided by Mira. Each day, she delved deeper into her soul, uncovering forgotten memories and unspoken desires. She sketched the trees, the pond, and the ethereal light, feeling her creativity flow like never before. She learned that the Soul Grove was more than just a place; it was a mirror of her inner world, a space where she could heal and understand herself fully.

One evening, as they sat by the pond, Mira shared the story of the Grove. "Long ago, this forest was home to an ancient tribe that understood the importance of connecting with one's soul. They created this sanctuary to help each other find their true paths. Over time, the tribe vanished, but the Grove remained, waiting for seekers like you."

Ellie realized that her journey to Everwood was not just about finding inspiration for her art; it was about finding herself. The Soul Grove had given her the gift of clarity and purpose. She knew now that her art was not just about creating beautiful images, but about expressing the truths she discovered within her soul.

As her time in the Grove came to an end, Mira gave Ellie a parting gift—a small, crystal pendant shaped like a heart. "This will remind you of your sacred soul place," she said. "Whenever you feel lost, hold it close, and you will find your way back to yourself."

Ellie returned to Everwood with a newfound sense of peace and purpose. She continued to create, her art now infused with the profound truths she had uncovered. And every so often, she would return to the Soul Grove, her sanctuary, to reconnect with her essence and the timeless wisdom of the ancient forest.

The legend of the Soul Grove lived on in Ellie's work, inspiring others to seek their own sacred soul places. The Grove, with its serene beauty and ethereal light, remained a beacon for those who were ready to embark on the journey of self-discovery, whispering its timeless message to all who listened: "Find your sacred soul place."

CHAPTER : THE FINAL JOURNEY: ANGEL ESCORT

The human sat in a quiet room, their thoughts heavy with questions about the mystery of death. The air was still, but within their heart, they sensed the familiar stir of the soul, ever present, ever patient. The soul spoke, its voice calm and reassuring, yet carrying the weight of profound truth.

"Death has always frightened you," it began gently, acknowledging the human's unspoken fears. "But it is not an end, only a transition—a journey from one state of being to another. And you are not alone in this journey. Angels, messengers of the divine, often come to escort souls beyond the veil."

The human's mind flooded with images of angels, luminous and serene, as they asked, "Is that really true? Do angels come to guide us when we die? Or is it just something we tell ourselves to feel less afraid?"

"Let me show you what I know," the soul replied. Its voice softened, weaving a sense of peace. "This idea is not born of wishful thinking. Across many traditions and teachings, there is a shared understanding: angels stand at the threshold between life and death, guiding souls with love and care. Their role is one of compassion, not judgment."

The soul paused, letting the human settle into their thoughts before continuing. "Take the Qur'an, for example," it began. "In Islam, angels are described as escorts for the righteous and the wicked alike, though their manner changes depending on the life the soul has lived. For the virtuous, angels of mercy bring comfort, saying: 'Peace be upon you; enter Paradise for what you used to do.' But for those who stray, the angels' presence can be more severe, reflecting the soul's own struggles and regrets."

The human nodded, remembering the reverence and solemnity with which death was spoken of in many cultures. "I've heard about the Angel of Death in Islam—Azrael, isn't it? Is he like the grim reaper, or is he different?"

"Azrael," the soul confirmed, "is one of the most recognized figures of transition in Islamic tradition. But he is not a figure to be feared. He is a collector of souls, gently separating the soul from the body and delivering it to its destination. For the faithful, his presence is a sign of divine care, while for others, he reflects the choices they have made."

The human's thoughts wandered to other texts, remembering fragments of stories. "What about Dante's Divine Comedy?" they asked. "I remember something about angels leading souls to heaven. Does that reflect a deeper truth, too?"

"It does," the soul said. "Dante described angels as celestial guides, beings of pure light who show souls the way to Paradise. In his work, angels are compassionate and nurturing, eager to see souls ascend. They are intermediaries between the mortal and the divine, ensuring that no soul becomes lost in the vastness of the afterlife."

"But it's not just Islam or Dante," the soul continued. "Think of other traditions. In Christianity, angels are described as both messengers and protectors, often appearing at the moment of death to guide the soul. The Book of Luke speaks of Lazarus, the beggar, being carried by angels to Abraham's bosom—a place of rest and peace. It is a powerful image of care and guidance."

The human thought about the stories they had grown up hearing, tales of loved ones speaking of angels before they passed. "I've heard people say they've seen angels at the end of their lives," they said hesitantly. "Even those who didn't believe in them before. Is that common?"

"Very," the soul affirmed. "In moments of transition, the veil between this world and the next thins. Many souls perceive angels near, their presence providing peace and reassurance. This is why so many describe deathbed visions—glimpses of radiant beings or loved ones already passed. It is the divine's way of ensuring no one crosses the threshold alone."

"But what happens next?" the human asked, their voice quieter now. "Once the angels come, where do they take us? What is it like?"

"That," the soul said gently, "depends on the soul's journey. The afterlife is vast and varied, with realms shaped by divine will and the soul's readiness. Some souls are guided to places of healing, resting in the care of angels until they are ready for what comes next. Others may ascend directly to higher planes, their lessons on Earth complete."

"And the others?" the human asked hesitantly, fearing the answer.

"For those who struggle, the angels' role is one of accountability," the soul explained. "They do not punish, but they guide the soul to face its choices. In Dante's vision, this might mean entering Purgatory, a place of refinement and growth. In Islamic teaching, it might involve a journey through the barzakh—a realm between worlds where the soul reflects and prepares for the Day of Judgment. But even here, the angels' presence is one of care, urging the soul toward redemption and understanding."

The human sat in silence, absorbing the magnitude of these words. "It sounds... so much bigger than I ever imagined," they admitted. "And the angels... they're there for all of us? No matter what?"

"Yes," the soul assured them. "Angels do not come to condemn. They come to guide. Their light is constant, even when the soul falters. They are reminders of divine love, escorting each of us back to where we belong."

"Can you tell me more?" the human asked, curiosity overtaking their fear. "Are there stories that show this? Not just in religious texts, but real ones?"

The soul smiled, as though remembering countless tales. "There are many," it said. "Consider the near-death experiences people often describe. Many speak of beings of light who greet them with warmth, love, and reassurance. These beings are often recognized as angels, though their names may differ. Some recount hearing music, feeling as though they were being carried, or seeing a golden pathway lit by radiant figures."

The human thought of a friend who had once described such an experience after surviving a car accident. "She said she felt weightless, like she was floating, and there was someone—something—there, telling her she'd be okay," they recalled.

"Exactly," the soul said. "Angels are not bound by physical form, but their presence is unmistakable. They guide the soul gently, showing it what it needs to see. Even those who return to life often carry the memory of their touch, a reassurance that they are never truly alone."

The soul's tone grew softer now, sensing the human's growing acceptance. "Death is not something to be feared," it said. "When the time comes, you will find yourself surrounded by light, love, and guidance. The angels will be there—not as strangers, but as companions who have walked with you all along."

The human felt a tear slip down their cheek, a mix of gratitude and awe. "It's beautiful," they whispered. "To think that even at the end, there is love waiting for us."

The soul smiled within them, a warm and steady presence. "It has always been there," it said. "And it always will be."

CHAPTER: SOUL PROTECTORS: ANGELS' ROLE IN THE AFTERLIFE

The human sat in a quiet space of introspection, their mind circling the ultimate questions: What happens after this life? Is there truly a judgment, a reckoning? The soul, ever patient, stirred in response, its voice steady, resonant with timeless wisdom.

"You wonder what awaits you beyond this life," the soul began, sensing the weight of the human's thoughts. "What judgment might come. Let us explore this together—not with fear, but with curiosity and trust."

The human nodded, leaning inward. "I've read about it in so many traditions—the idea that there's a moment when everything about us is weighed, measured. It feels... overwhelming. Like I might not measure up."

The soul's presence softened, an embrace of calm around the human's restless thoughts. "Judgment is not about punishment or failure," it assured. "It is a mirror, held up with love and clarity, to show the soul its journey. Angels often stand at the heart of this moment—not as harsh arbiters, but as witnesses, guides, and reflections of divine ideals."

The soul began to weave its narrative, drawing on the threads of many traditions.

"In the Book of Revelation, angels play pivotal roles in the judgment of souls. They sound the trumpets that herald the end times and guide the faithful to their place in eternity. They are not there to condemn, but to ensure that the divine plan unfolds with precision and justice. In one passage, John describes seeing 'another angel flying in midair, and he had the eternal gospel to proclaim to those who live on the earth...' Angels serve as messengers of truth, reminding souls of their purpose and accountability."

The human closed their eyes, imagining these celestial beings, radiant and steadfast. "They seem so perfect," they murmured. "Do they ever falter?"

"No," the soul replied gently. "Angels are embodiments of divine will. They are the pure ideal of what the soul strives to become—not through comparison or competition, but as an inspiration. They remind us of our highest potential, of the light that already exists within us."

The human's thoughts shifted to a vivid image from their memory. "I remember learning about the ancient Egyptians," they said, "and how they believed a soul's heart was weighed against a feather. If the heart was heavy with wrongs, the soul couldn't move forward."

The soul's voice took on a tone of reflection. "Yes, the weighing of the heart is one of the earliest depictions of judgment. In Egyptian mythology, the goddess Ma'at, representing truth and order, oversees this process. The feather is her symbol, a representation of the soul's harmony with universal laws. Angels in other traditions fulfill a similar role—not as accusers, but as facilitators of balance and truth."

The human frowned. "But what if the heart is heavy? What happens then?"

"Then the soul learns," the soul replied simply. "Judgment is not an end but a transition. In many traditions, including Christianity and Islam, angels guide souls through purification. For some, this may mean Purgatory—a realm of refinement described in Dante's Divine Comedy. For others, it is the reckoning of the barzakh, the intermediate state in Islamic eschatology. Always, the angels are there, not to condemn but to support the soul's progress toward the divine."

"Are angels always watching us?" the human asked, an edge of discomfort in their voice.

The soul offered a sense of reassurance. "Angels are not spies," it said. "In Islamic teaching, they are described as recorders—Kiraman Katibin—who note every deed, good and bad. Their role is not to judge, but to reflect. They hold up a mirror to the soul at the time of reckoning, allowing it to see itself clearly."

The human considered this, their discomfort easing. "So, they're more like keepers of truth?"

"Precisely," the soul affirmed. "In the Qur'an, these angels are described as noble and faithful, unerring in their record. Their presence is not meant to invoke fear, but accountability. They remind us that our lives are sacred stories, written moment by moment."

The soul's tone shifted, inviting the human to think more deeply. "But angels are more than recorders or escorts. They are symbols of what the soul aspires to become. Their purity reflects the potential within every human being to align with the divine."

The human tilted their head, intrigued. "You mean they're not just separate beings—they're like... mirrors for us?"

"Exactly," the soul said. "In many philosophical traditions, angels represent virtues—truth, compassion, courage, and humility. The poet Rainer Maria Rilke once wrote in his Duino Elegies, 'Every angel is terrifying.' Not because they wish us harm, but because they represent the vastness of what we are called to become. They challenge us to rise, to grow, to step into our highest selves."

"But what happens," the human asked hesitantly, "if a soul falls short? If the judgment shows a life full of mistakes?"

The soul was quiet for a moment, a pause filled with compassion. "No soul is beyond redemption," it said finally. "Judgment is not a sentence; it is a revelation. The divine does not seek to punish but to heal. Angels guide the soul toward understanding, helping it see where love was withheld, where choices were made in fear. And they walk with it as it chooses again."

The human felt a swell of emotion, a mixture of relief and awe. "So, even in judgment, there's love?"

"Always," the soul replied. "Judgment is a form of grace, a chance to see oneself through the eyes of the divine. Angels are there to ensure that no soul walks this path alone, that every journey is met with compassion and hope."

The soul shared stories of those who had glimpsed this truth in life. "Consider near-death experiences," it said. "Many describe a moment of review—a life flashing before their eyes. But they also describe a presence, often interpreted as angelic, that offers comfort and understanding. These beings do not judge harshly; they illuminate the soul's choices, helping it see with clarity and love."

The human thought of a story they'd once heard, of a man who had nearly drowned and later spoke of a radiant being showing him his life. "He said it wasn't about shame," they murmured, "but about learning. Like he was being shown how to do better."

"That is the essence of judgment," the soul confirmed. "A chance to grow, to align more closely with the divine. Angels are the facilitators of this process, offering their light to guide the way."

The human sat quietly, the enormity of the soul's words settling around them. "So, angels are more than we think," they said finally. "Not just beings who deliver messages or protect us, but... ideals. Reminders of what we could be."

"Yes," the soul said simply. "They are both guides and reflections. They call you not to perfection, but to authenticity. To become the truest expression of your divine essence."

The human felt a deep sense of peace, as though a weight they hadn't known they carried had been lifted. "Maybe judgment isn't something to fear after all," they said softly.

The soul's presence radiated warmth, a gentle affirmation. "No, it is not," it said. "It is a step on the journey, guided always by love, with angels lighting the way."

CHAPTER: REINCARNATION AND THE CYCLE OF SOULS WITH ANGELS

The human sat quietly, their thoughts churning with questions that seemed to spiral endlessly. "If the soul doesn't simply end after one life," they mused aloud, "what happens next? How does it move on—or come back?"

The soul stirred, its voice both steady and compassionate. "You are speaking of reincarnation," it said. "The cycle of lives through which a soul journeys, learning, growing, evolving."

The human leaned in, curious. "But where do angels fit into that? If they guide us in death, do they also play a role in rebirth?"

The soul's presence grew warmer, inviting reflection. "Indeed, they do. Angels are eternal companions of the soul, present not just in moments of departure but in the transitions between realms. Let us explore this together."

The soul began its explanation, weaving together threads of various spiritual traditions.

"Reincarnation is the belief that the soul returns to the physical world through successive lives," it said. "In Hinduism and Buddhism, this is called samsara—the cycle of birth, death, and rebirth. It is a process of learning, a path toward liberation from earthly attachments. Angels, though not always named directly, are often present as guides and facilitators in this journey."

The human tilted their head. "Facilitators? You mean they help decide where the soul goes next?"

"In some traditions, yes," the soul replied. "Consider the Tibetan Book of the Dead, which describes a transitional state known as the bardo. It is said that luminous beings—reminiscent of angels—appear to guide the soul through this liminal space, helping it find its next incarnation or achieve liberation."

The human's brow furrowed in thought. "So, angels aren't just about endings. They're part of beginnings, too."

"Precisely," the soul affirmed. "Just as they guide souls through death, they also shepherd them into new lives, ensuring that each transition serves the soul's highest purpose."

"Reincarnation," the soul continued, "is deeply tied to the concept of karma—the accumulated actions and their consequences across lifetimes. Angels, in some interpretations, act as stewards of this cosmic balance. They ensure that the circumstances of a soul's next life align with the lessons it needs to learn."

The human thought of the weight of their choices, the ripple effects of their actions. "So, angels don't judge us, but they... arrange things? Based on what we need?"

The soul's tone was gentle. "Yes. In the Bhagavad Gita, it is said, 'As a person sheds worn-out garments and wears new ones, likewise, the soul casts off its worn-out body and enters a new one.' Angels, or divine emissaries, ensure that this transition honors the soul's unique path. They are not arbiters of punishment but facilitators of growth."

The human nodded slowly, imagining these celestial beings weaving threads of fate, connecting lives with purpose and care. "It's comforting," they murmured, "to think we're never alone in this process."

The soul shifted, its voice now colored with stories and examples. "In many cultures, angels or angel-like beings appear in narratives of reincarnation. For instance, in Jewish mysticism, there is the Angel Lailah, who is said to guide the soul into the physical world. She whispers divine wisdom into the ear of the unborn, though it is forgotten at birth. Her role is to help the soul remember its purpose."

The human's eyes widened. "I've heard of that before—the idea that we're born with all this knowledge, but we lose it."

"Yes," the soul replied. "And the journey of life is about rediscovering that wisdom. Angels like Lailah are there to ensure the soul's entry into life is guided by the divine plan, even if the human mind cannot yet comprehend it."

The soul then spoke of Buddhist beliefs. "In Tibetan Buddhism, deities and luminous beings appear to the soul in the bardo, offering opportunities for enlightenment or guidance toward reincarnation. These beings are often interpreted as angelic in their purpose—they are compassionate helpers, offering the soul clarity and choice."

The human leaned forward, a question pressing on their mind. "But what about free will? If angels are guiding the process, do we have any say in where we go next?"

The soul's tone was thoughtful. "Free will and divine guidance coexist. Before reincarnating, the soul often participates in choosing the circumstances of its next life. This is not a random act but a deliberate decision made with the assistance of angels or spiritual guides. They help the soul understand its karmic needs and the opportunities for growth that each life presents."

The human's expression softened, a sense of awe dawning. "So, we're not just thrown into random lives. There's purpose behind it all."

"There is always purpose," the soul said gently. "Even when it is not immediately apparent. Angels act as stewards of this purpose, ensuring that the soul's journey is aligned with its highest good."

The human sighed, their thoughts turning to the idea of endless lives, endless lessons. "Does it ever end?" they asked quietly. "This cycle of reincarnation?"

The soul's presence grew serene, as if smiling. "Yes," it said. "The cycle ends when the soul achieves liberation—when it has learned all it needs to learn, when it is no longer bound by attachment or illusion. In Hinduism, this is called moksha; in Buddhism, it is nirvana. At this point, the soul merges with the divine, returning to its source."

The human felt a pang of hope. "And angels? Are they still there, even then?"

"Always," the soul replied. "For angels are not bound by the cycles of life and death. They exist beyond time, serving as eternal companions and guides. Whether you are taking your first breath in a new life or your last breath before liberation, they are with you."

The human sat quietly, absorbing the soul's words. "It's a lot to take in," they admitted. "But it makes sense—that angels are part of all of it. Beginnings, endings, and everything in between."

"They are," the soul affirmed. "They are the threads that connect each chapter of your journey. They remind you of your purpose, help you carry your burdens, and celebrate your triumphs. Through every incarnation, they are a constant presence, ensuring that you never walk alone."

The human smiled, a sense of peace settling over them. "It's comforting to know they're there, even when I can't see them."

The soul's presence radiated warmth, a gentle affirmation. "Trust in their guidance," it said. "And trust in the wisdom of your journey. Every life, every lesson, every transition is part of the great tapestry of your evolution. And angels are always there, weaving light into your path."

CHAPTER: THE INFINITE SELF: THE MYSTERY

The human sat quietly, eyes closed, lost in contemplation. "Soul," they whispered into the stillness, "is it possible that my consciousness—this sense of me—is really... you?"

The soul, patient and ever-present, stirred gently in response. "Ah, my curious friend," it said, its voice soft yet resonant. "You're beginning to see the connection. Shall we unravel this mystery together?"

The human smiled faintly. "Please. Start at the beginning. What is consciousness, really?"

"Consciousness," the soul began, "is the essence of your awareness. It is the inner stream of thoughts, emotions, and perceptions that shapes your understanding of the world and your place in it. When you say, 'I am,' you are speaking directly from this sacred space. But here's the deeper truth: your consciousness is not just a function of your mind; it is the very fabric of your soul."

The human's curiosity deepened. "So, my thoughts and feelings—my awareness—are you?"

"Yes," the soul replied. "I am the seat of your self-awareness. When you reflect on your dreams or dive into the depths of your emotions, you're exploring the vastness of me. I carry your memories, your lessons, and the threads of your past and present woven into the tapestry of your being."

The human paused, letting the words settle. "But how can something as intangible as consciousness be part of something eternal, like you? Doesn't it end with the body?"

The soul radiated warmth, a smile felt rather than seen. "Ah, that's the illusion of the material world. Your body is a vessel, yes, and your brain helps process the physical experience. But your consciousness—the essence of you—is not confined to this flesh. Think of it as light shining through a prism. The body is the prism, and I am the light. Even when the prism shatters, the light continues to exist, undimmed and infinite."

The human's thoughts drifted to moments in life that had felt inexplicably profound. "What about those flashes of intuition? Or times when I just knew something without understanding why?"

The soul's energy shimmered with understanding. "Those are my whispers," it said. "Moments when the veil between us thins, and you feel the truth of your being. Archangel Raziel often aids in these moments, helping you access divine knowledge hidden within the depths of your consciousness. These flashes are reminders that you are more than a collection of thoughts—you are connected to something eternal."

"Is that why people describe leaving their bodies during near-death experiences?" the human asked. "Is that me—my soul—stepping outside?"

"Exactly," the soul affirmed. "When the body quiets, even momentarily, you catch a glimpse of your true nature. In those moments, consciousness transcends the physical realm, revealing the boundless essence of the soul. Archangel Azrael, the angel of transitions, often walks with souls during these journeys, ensuring they feel safe and guided."

The human's gaze lifted toward an invisible horizon. "So, if consciousness is you, then it's immortal?"

"Yes," the soul said gently. "When the body falls away, I carry your consciousness forward, just as I have through lifetimes before this one. Each life is a chapter in the great story of your existence. I am the keeper of your essence, the thread that links all your experiences, past, present, and future."

The human's thoughts shifted to a broader perspective. "And what about others? Does this mean we're all connected somehow?"

"Beautifully so," the soul answered. "Each of us is a unique note in the symphony of existence. While you are distinct, you are also part of a greater whole. Your consciousness resonates with the collective soul of the universe. Archangel Metatron, who bridges heaven and earth, often facilitates this understanding, showing souls how their individual light contributes to the greater harmony."

The human leaned back, marveling at the intricate dance between individuality and unity. "Science tries to explain consciousness—neurons firing, the brain working—but it feels like something more."

"It is," the soul agreed. "Science glimpses pieces of the truth. Quantum theories, for example, hint at consciousness as a fundamental aspect of reality, interconnected across time and space. These discoveries align with spiritual teachings, where consciousness is seen as the divine thread weaving through all creation. When you meditate or practice mindfulness, you're not just calming your mind—you're touching the divine within."

The human exhaled slowly, feeling the enormity of it all. "If this is true, what does it mean for how I live?"

"It means living authentically," the soul said, its voice both grounding and uplifting. "If your consciousness is your soul, then every moment is sacred. Listen to your intuition, honor your inner voice, and align your actions with your deepest values. Live as though each breath connects you to the infinite, because it does."

"And what about death?" the human asked softly.

The soul's presence grew tender. "Death is not an end," it said. "It is a transition, a return to the fullness of your essence. Your consciousness—your soul—steps beyond the physical form, continuing the journey. Archangel Azrael is there to guide, ensuring that this passage is one of peace and understanding."

The human sat quietly, a profound peace settling over them. "So, my consciousness—my soul—is both me and something much greater."

"Exactly," the soul said. "You are the light, the song, the infinite thread of existence. Embrace this truth, and you will navigate life with greater clarity, courage, and love."

In that moment, surrounded by unseen angels and the infinite depth of their soul, the human felt a quiet certainty. They were not merely a body, not merely a mind, but an eternal consciousness—a soul forever intertwined with the universe. And with that, they began to live with a newfound grace, knowing they were part of something timeless, something beautiful, and something endlessly profound.

STORY: ECHOES OF THE MIND

In the heart of the bustling city of Havenwood, beneath the glow of neon lights and the hum of endless traffic, a mystery was unfolding that defied the boundaries of life and death. Dr. Lydia Morgan, a renowned neuroscientist, was about to encounter a truth that would challenge her understanding of consciousness and the very essence of the soul.

It began on a rainy Tuesday evening. Lydia was working late in her lab at the Havenwood Institute of Neuroscience, her mind engrossed in a complex study on brain wave patterns. The rhythmic tapping of rain against the window provided a soothing backdrop to her focused concentration.

Suddenly, a cold draft swept through the room, and Lydia looked up, startled. The door, which she was certain she had closed, stood ajar. She frowned, glancing around the empty corridor. Shaking her head, she returned to her work, chalking it up to a faulty latch.

Minutes later, the temperature dropped noticeably. Lydia shivered, pulling her lab coat tighter around her. Out of the corner of her eye, she saw a flicker of movement. Her heart raced as she turned, but there was nothing there. Just the shadows cast by the dim lab lights.

As she turned back to her work, her computer screen flickered, and a series of strange, rhythmic patterns appeared—patterns she had never seen before. They seemed almost...alive. Intrigued, Lydia began to record the data, unaware that this was only the beginning.

The next day, Lydia couldn't shake the feeling that she was being watched. Her colleagues noticed her distraction and tried to coax her into joining them for lunch, but she declined, her mind preoccupied with the previous night's events.

Returning to her lab, Lydia found an old book on her desk—a book she had never seen before. The cover was worn, and the pages yellowed with age. It was titled "The Echoes of the Mind: A Study on Consciousness and the Soul." Intrigued, she began to read, discovering it was written by Dr. Evelyn Shaw, a scientist who had mysteriously disappeared over two decades ago.

The book detailed experiments on brain wave patterns and their correlation with spiritual phenomena. It spoke of a theory that consciousness was not just a product of the brain but an eternal entity—a soul that transcended physical existence. Lydia was skeptical but fascinated.

That night, as she lay in bed, Lydia couldn't stop thinking about the book. Could it be possible that consciousness was more than just a neural phenomenon? Could it be...eternal?

Determined to find answers, Lydia delved into Dr. Shaw's work. She discovered that Shaw had been on the verge of a breakthrough when she vanished. According to the records, Shaw had been experimenting with a device that could allegedly capture the essence of consciousness.

Lydia decided to recreate Shaw's experiments, hoping to understand the connection between brain waves and the soul. As she replicated the setup described in the book, she felt a strange mix of excitement and dread.

Late one night, while working with the device, Lydia noticed a pattern similar to the one that had appeared on her computer screen. The patterns seemed to pulse with a rhythm, almost like a heartbeat. She felt a sudden, overwhelming presence in the room, as if she were not alone.

Her heart pounded as she heard a faint whisper, barely audible, saying, "Find me." Lydia spun around, but the room was empty. The voice had sounded familiar, almost like her own,

Lydia's obsession with the experiment began to take a toll. She spent countless hours in the lab, her nights filled with strange dreams and whispers that seemed to guide her. Her colleagues grew concerned, but Lydia brushed off their worries, convinced she was on the brink of a monumental discovery.

SOUL PROTECTORS

One night, as she pored over Shaw's notes, Lydia stumbled upon a personal journal entry. In it, Shaw described a patient named Eleanor, who had experienced vivid dreams of past lives. Shaw believed Eleanor's consciousness was accessing memories from previous incarnations, suggesting that the soul carried experiences beyond a single lifetime.

Curious, Lydia decided to track down Eleanor. She discovered that Eleanor was now living in a remote part of the city, a recluse known for her eccentricities. Lydia visited her, hoping to find clues that would tie Shaw's work to her own experiences.

Eleanor, a frail woman with piercing blue eyes, greeted Lydia with a knowing smile. "I've been expecting you," she said cryptically. Over tea, Eleanor shared her experiences of past lives and the sense of an eternal consciousness that transcended her physical existence.

"You're closer to the truth than you realize," Eleanor said. "Our consciousness is our soul, an echo of all that we have been and all that we will be."

Armed with Eleanor's insights, Lydia returned to her lab, determined to prove that consciousness was indeed an eternal soul. She continued her experiments, pushing the boundaries of science and spirituality.

One stormy night, as lightning flashed and thunder rumbled, Lydia activated the device once more. This time, the patterns on the screen were more vibrant, more alive than ever. The room filled with an otherworldly light, and Lydia felt herself being drawn into the device.

Suddenly, she found herself in a vast, ethereal landscape, a place beyond time and space. There, she encountered a figure—Dr. Evelyn Shaw. Shaw's presence was serene, her form luminous.

"Welcome, Lydia," Shaw said with a gentle smile. "You've found the truth. Consciousness is not bound by the physical world. It is our soul, eternal and infinite."

Lydia felt a profound sense of peace and understanding. She realized that her journey had been guided by her own soul, an eternal consciousness seeking to reveal its true nature.

As she returned to the physical world, Lydia knew she had to share her discovery. She published her findings, merging science and spirituality in a groundbreaking work that challenged conventional beliefs about consciousness and the soul.

Lydia's work revolutionized the field of neuroscience, inspiring a new generation of scientists and spiritual seekers. Her book, "The Echoes of the Mind: The Soul's Journey," became a beacon of hope and a testament to the eternal nature of consciousness.

And as for Lydia, she continued her journey, exploring the mysteries of the mind and soul, knowing that she was part of something far greater than herself—an eternal consciousness, an echo of the infinite.

CHAPTER: ANGELS AS ART INSPIRATION

The human sat at the edge of their bed, their gaze wandering toward a framed print on the wall—a painting of an angel, luminous and serene, with outstretched wings enveloping a group of vulnerable figures. They sighed. "Why do angels show up so often in art, music, and stories? It's like they've always been there, across centuries, cultures, and mediums."

The soul stirred within them, its voice calm and resonant. "Because angels are archetypes," it said, "symbols of something eternal within you. They embody hope, protection, and the connection to the divine. Artists, poets, and composers have always reached for what is timeless, and angels stand at the intersection of the seen and the unseen, making them the perfect subject to capture the ineffable."

The soul began its tale with the Renaissance, a period when angels took center stage in European art. "Consider Michelangelo's Sistine Chapel," it said. "There, angels hover between heaven and earth, their forms simultaneously human and divine. They symbolize the guardianship of humanity's spiritual potential, as if reminding you that the soul is always cradled by higher forces."

The human nodded, recalling the frescoes they'd studied in school. "And those cherubs—Raphael's, right? The ones on postcards and Christmas cards?"

"Yes," the soul replied. "Raphael's Cherubim from the Sistine Madonna are iconic. Though small, they carry immense significance. Their curious, pensive expressions capture the paradox of angelic presence—playful yet wise, otherworldly yet intimately connected to human concerns. They have become a shorthand for divine guardianship in popular culture."

The soul spoke next of Fra Angelico, a monk-artist whose works were imbued with devotion. "His angels are luminous and serene, often depicted in vibrant golds and blues. They embody the purity and light of divine guidance, reinforcing the idea that angels are protectors of the soul's journey through this world and beyond."

"Angels have also soared across the pages of literature," the soul continued. "John Milton's Paradise Lost offers one of the most profound explorations of angelic roles. While some angels in his epic are warriors and messengers, others serve as guardians of humanity's spiritual potential. Think of the Archangel Michael, who guides Adam and Eve after the Fall, showing them a vision of redemption."

The human frowned, trying to recall. "But isn't Milton's depiction kind of dark? Angels wielding swords and banishing humanity?"

The soul's voice was understanding. "True, but even in their sternness, they act out of love and duty to the divine order. Their role is not to punish but to guide—sometimes through difficult truths. Michael's actions remind humanity of its resilience and capacity for growth, even in exile. Angels, in Milton's world, are mirrors of the soul's potential for redemption."

The conversation turned to more recent works. "In Rainer Maria Rilke's Duino Elegies, angels are ethereal, awe-inspiring figures that reflect humanity's yearning for transcendence," the soul said. "Rilke writes, 'Every angel is terrifying.' His angels challenge the reader to confront the vastness of existence and the divine, underscoring that angelic guidance isn't always gentle—it's transformative."

"And music?" the human asked. "How do composers bring angels to life in sound?"

The soul seemed to hum, its tone resonant with joy. "Music is a natural language for angels, as it transcends words and speaks directly to the spirit. Consider Handel's Messiah, particularly the Hallelujah Chorus. While not explicitly about angels, the work evokes celestial grandeur, as if the choir itself were composed of angelic voices."

The soul also mentioned Franz Schubert's Ave Maria. "This piece, often associated with angelic devotion, encapsulates the essence of divine protection and grace. It is a prayer, yes, but also a musical embodiment of the soul's longing for the guardianship of higher powers."

The human closed their eyes, imagining the soaring notes. "It's like you can feel angels in the music," they said softly.

"Yes," the soul replied. "In the crescendos and harmonies, you sense the presence of something greater—a reminder that angels are never far, even in sound."

Contemporary Art: The Angelic Metaphor

"And what about today?" the human asked. "Do angels still show up in modern art?"

The soul answered with enthusiasm. "Absolutely. Artists continue to reinterpret angels for contemporary audiences, often blending traditional symbolism with modern themes. Consider Marc Chagall, whose paintings often feature floating, dreamlike angels. They are not bound by religious doctrine but serve as universal symbols of hope, love, and transcendence."

The soul also pointed to films like Wings of Desire by Wim Wenders. "In this cinematic masterpiece, angels walk among humans, unseen but deeply present, observing their struggles and offering silent guidance. It's a poignant reminder that angels are not just guardians of the soul but witnesses to the full breadth of human experience."

In literature, authors like Paulo Coelho have used angels as metaphors for inner transformation. "In The Valkyries, Coelho explores the idea that angels help us confront our fears and embrace our true selves," the soul said. "It's a contemporary take on an ancient theme, showing that angelic guidance is as relevant now as it was in the past."

The human's expression grew thoughtful. "It seems like angels are more than just beings—they're symbols, too."

"Precisely," the soul said. "Angels often serve as metaphors for higher guidance, the ideal self, or the divine spark within. When artists depict angels, they are often exploring humanity's connection to something greater. This is why angelic imagery resonates so deeply—it speaks to the soul's innate longing for transcendence and protection."

The soul paused, its voice softening. "Whether in the brushstrokes of a Renaissance painting, the words of a poet, or the chords of a symphony, angels remind you that you are never alone. They are the guardians of your soul, appearing in forms that resonate most deeply with your heart and imagination."

The human looked back at the angelic painting on their wall. It no longer felt like a mere decoration. "I never realized how much history, meaning, and emotion was tied to angels in art," they said. "It's like they've been speaking to us all along, even when we didn't notice."

"They have," the soul replied gently. "Through every stroke of paint, every line of poetry, and every note of music, angels remind you of your connection to the divine. They are the eternal guardians of the soul, whispering of hope, light, and love—if only you have the ears to hear and the eyes to see."

The human smiled, feeling a new depth to the image before them. "Maybe that's the secret," they said. "Learning to see the angels all around us."

"Exactly," the soul agreed. "In art, in music, in life—they are always there, waiting to be recognized."

CHAPTER: PSYCHOLOGICAL AND PERSONAL VIEWS

The human settled into their favorite chair, a well-worn journal in hand. They had been reflecting on stories they'd heard—friends recounting inexplicable moments of clarity, strangers sharing tales of unseen forces intervening in their lives. "Are angels real?" they asked aloud. "Or are they just projections of our minds, symbols for something deeper within us?"

The soul stirred, its voice calm and contemplative. "Angels are real," it said, "but what 'real' means is often misunderstood. Sometimes, they are external presences—guides and protectors who walk unseen. Other times, they are reflections of your own psyche, archetypes of wisdom and strength. The truth is, they can be both, depending on what you need in the moment."

The soul's voice took on a tone of quiet reflection. "In psychology, angels are often understood as archetypes—universal symbols that reside in the collective unconscious, as Carl Jung described. They represent protection, guidance, and transcendence. When you imagine an angel, you may actually be accessing an inner part of yourself, a reservoir of strength and clarity."

The human frowned. "So, are angels just... me talking to myself?"

"Not quite," the soul replied. "Think of them as bridges. They connect your conscious mind to your deeper self, or even to the divine. When you encounter an angel in your dreams or thoughts, it may be your psyche's way of reminding you that you are protected, loved, and capable of rising above challenges."

The soul cited a famous example: "Jung himself spoke of the anima and animus—inner figures representing the soul's connection to greater truths. Angels, in many ways, serve a similar purpose. They guide you toward wholeness, urging you to integrate the fragmented parts of yourself into a cohesive, balanced being."

The human nodded slowly. "That makes sense. It's like they're symbolic protectors, whether they're literal beings or not."

The conversation shifted as the soul began recounting real stories. "Take, for instance, the experience of Lorna Byrne, author of Angels in My Hair. She describes seeing angels from a young age, beings who comforted her and helped her navigate challenges. Her accounts have inspired millions, even skeptics, because they speak to something universal: the longing to feel watched over and supported."

The human tapped their pen against the journal. "Her story is beautiful, but what about people who aren't sure they've seen angels? What about those subtle moments that don't involve glowing figures or wings?"

The soul smiled in its way. "Angels often appear in quieter forms. A stranger offering help at just the right time. A dream that brings clarity. A sudden, inexplicable sense of peace in a moment of chaos. Consider the story of Elizabeth Gilbert, who wrote about hearing a voice during a deep depression. It wasn't dramatic—just a quiet directive to 'go home.' She later credited that moment with saving her life, whether it was an angel or her inner wisdom."

The human added a note in their journal: Sometimes angels whisper.

The soul then turned to the modern field of psychology. "Therapists and scholars often frame angelic encounters as manifestations of the inner guide—a concept popularized by Carl Rogers and other humanistic psychologists. These inner guides help individuals access deeper truths, offering clarity and comfort in times of distress."

"Can you give me an example?" the human asked.

"Of course," the soul replied. "In Viktor Frankl's Man's Search for Meaning, he recounts moments in the concentration camps where he felt an overwhelming presence—something beyond himself—urging him to keep going. Frankl interpreted it as the essence of love, hope, and his connection to others. While he didn't describe it as an angel, the effect was the same. It was a force that protected his spirit and guided him toward survival."

The human considered this. "So angels might not always be literal beings, but their role is real—whether they come from inside us or beyond."

"Precisely," the soul said. "What matters isn't where they come from, but the transformation they inspire."

The soul encouraged the human to explore firsthand accounts. "Consider interviews with people who have experienced what they describe as angelic intervention. Some speak of near-death experiences where they saw radiant beings leading them toward light, only to be told it wasn't their time. Others recount waking dreams or visions where an angel offered wisdom that later proved transformative."

The soul mentioned one poignant story: "A woman once shared how she narrowly avoided a car accident because she 'heard' a voice tell her to slow down. She obeyed, only to see a collision happen just ahead of her. Was it her intuition? A guardian angel? She'll never know for sure, but the experience stayed with her as a reminder of unseen protection."

"Do skeptics believe any of this?" the human asked.

"Some skeptics argue that these experiences are merely coincidences or psychological phenomena," the soul said. "But even they acknowledge that such moments can have profound effects on people's lives. Whether angels are literal beings or symbolic projections, their impact is undeniable."

The soul continued, its tone softening. "In trauma therapy, angelic imagery is sometimes used to help individuals process their pain. Visualizing a protective presence can provide comfort and safety, allowing people to explore difficult emotions without feeling overwhelmed."

The human jotted down a note. "So, angels aren't just spiritual—they're practical, too."

"Exactly," the soul said. "They're a tool for healing, whether they manifest as external beings or inner archetypes."

The human set their journal aside, lost in thought. "It's incredible how versatile angels are," they said. "They can be symbols, guides, protectors—whatever we need them to be."

"They are mirrors of the soul," the soul replied. "When you call on them, you're calling on the best parts of yourself—the parts that are wise, compassionate, and connected to something greater. And whether they come from within or beyond, they remind you that you are never truly alone."

The human smiled. "I like that. Angels, real or symbolic, are about connection. To ourselves, to others, to something bigger."

The soul's presence grew warm. "Exactly. They are the guardians of your journey, whispering that you are loved, guided, and always protected—no matter how you choose to see them."

FINAL

The human sat in quiet contemplation, gazing at the flickering light of a candle on the table. The air felt still, charged with the weight of all they had explored. The soul, ever patient, stirred gently within, sensing the human's questions before they could even be spoken.

"You've guided me through so much," the human said softly. "I feel like I've touched something immense, something sacred. But now that we've reached the end, I wonder—what am I supposed to do with it all? How do I take what I've learned and make it... real?"

The soul's presence was steady, its voice warm with understanding. "That is the great question, isn't it? The wisdom you've gained, the stories of angels, the soul's journeys—they are not meant to stay here in this moment. They are seeds, and your life is the fertile ground in which they must grow."

The soul's voice softened, carrying the weight of countless lifetimes. "Angels are not just protectors of the soul; they are reminders. They remind you that you are part of something far greater than this single life, this single moment. Whether you've seen them in the brushstrokes of art, the quiet whispers of your intuition, or the profound guidance of another soul, their presence has always been there, weaving through your journey."

The human nodded, the memories vivid now. Angels as messengers in dreams, as archetypes in the psyche, as figures in literature and art. Angels as escorts in life's transitions, as symbols of judgment, as companions through reincarnation's cycle. The vastness of it all left them breathless.

"Everything we've explored," the soul continued, "has pointed to one truth: You are deeply connected—to the divine, to the universe, and to others. Angels, in all their forms, help you remember that connection. They are not separate from you. They are within you, around you, and through you. Their purpose is to guide you toward your highest self and remind you of your eternal nature."

The human leaned forward, their voice quiet but urgent. "So how does this change how I live my life? How do I take this knowledge into the everyday?"

The soul answered with a calm certainty. "Begin by trusting the unseen. Not everything that shapes your path will be visible or tangible. Angels, whether you see them as external beings or reflections of your deepest wisdom, are always there. When you feel lost, remember that you are never truly alone. Ask for guidance. Trust your intuition. Lean into the moments that feel like whispers from something greater."

"And what about others?" the human asked.

"Treat them as if they, too, are guided," the soul said. "Everyone is on their own journey, accompanied by their own unseen forces. Be patient. Be compassionate. Offer kindness freely, for you may be an angel to someone without even realizing it."

The human closed their eyes, letting the soul's words settle. "It's humbling," they said. "To think of angels not just as otherworldly beings, but as part of this web of connection. It makes me feel... smaller, but also bigger."

"That is the paradox," the soul said with a smile in its tone. "You are a part of something infinite, and yet you are profoundly significant. Angels are the threads that weave these truths together, guiding you back to the knowledge that you are both the seeker and the sacred."

The soul grew quiet for a moment, letting the stillness take root. Then it spoke one last time. "Take this knowledge and let it shape you. Reflect on the stories and lessons we've uncovered. Look for angels in unexpected places—in art, in nature, in the stranger who smiles at you when you're weary. And most of all, remember that you carry within you a piece of the divine. Nurture it, listen to it, and let it guide you."

The candle flickered, its light steady even as the flame danced. The human opened their eyes, a sense of peace washing over them.

"I think I understand," they said. "Angels aren't just protectors of the soul—they're part of the journey itself. They remind me who I am, where I've been, and where I'm going."

The soul's voice was full of quiet joy. "Exactly. And now, your journey continues. The book may end, but the lessons, the connection—they will go with you. You are the guardian of your own soul, and yet, you are never without guidance. Trust in that, and walk forward with courage."

The human smiled, a deep, abiding calm settling within. They blew out the candle, but the light remained—illuminating the path ahead, where angels awaited in every shadow and every gleam.

About the Author

Jodi Dehn is an intuitive empath, paranormal investigator, motivational speaker, life coach, published author, ordained pastor and former U.S. Army Chaplain. She had her first angel encounter at age four, which planted the seeds for her decades-long work as an angel lightworker. Her work with angels and her military experiences led to the creation of Survivor Angels.

Jodi's passionate goals for Survivor Angels are to strengthen and support trauma survivors and others who struggle with life's challenges. Through Survivor Angels, Jodi offers loving support to help you escape life's negative energies, and engage positive abilities and gifts that have always been present.

She earned her Master of Divinity degree from Luther Seminary in Saint Paul, MN in 1996. She lives in Minnesota.

Survivor Angels hosts a daily blog (Cerebrations), weekly podcast, and other celestial resources. You can find Jodi's angel work at chaplainjodi.me and Survivor Angels - Chaplain Jodi on Facebook, Instagram, TikTok, Pinterest, YouTube, and wherever you listen to your podcasts.

Read more at https://www.chaplainjodi.me/.

www.ingramcontent.com/pod-product-compliance
Lightning Source LLC
Chambersburg PA
CBHW020157090426
42734CB00008B/854